Additional Praise

"What an exciting new resource for school principals and other educational leaders. Lyman and her team have researched the latest developments in how brain science relates to learning. Leaders will find practical knowledge in this book. Read it and discover how to facilitate and support the best possible approaches to engaging diverse students and teachers in their own individual and collective learning journey." —**Margaret Grogan**, PhD, dean and professor of educational leadership and policy, College of Educational Studies, Chapman University

"Lyman's book is an important step in bringing brain science to school leadership in important and useful ways. Perhaps the most delightful part of this book is its breadth of principal work related to brain science, including everything from challenging the idea of fixed intelligence to content learning (including the arts in schools) to thinking carefully about principals' mindfulness. We are a better field for having this as a key resource!" —**George Theoharis**, PhD, professor and department chair of teaching and leadership, Syracuse University

"Principals who read this will be better able to support teachers and increase instructional effectiveness through an understanding of how learning occurs." —**Donna Wilson**, PhD, lead developer, Brain-Based Teaching programs, Fischler School of Education, Nova Southeastern University

"The responsibilities of principals are complex and expanding, and *Brain Science for Principals* supplies them with information they need. In this book written by practitioners, principals new to the profession will find current information and applicable strategies they likely did not receive as part of their training. Seasoned principals will recognize many of the ideas posed from previous information on child development and student motivation, but with enriched and updated information from neuroscience. All principals will gain new perspectives of students' diverse academic, physical, and emotional needs, and have the scientific backing they need to create environments where students learn in brain-friendly ways, experience subjects that motivate and enrich them, and are less constrained by old notions of who they are or who they can become." —**Debby Zambo**, PhD, associate director of the Carnegie Project on the Education Doctorate (CPED); professor emerita, Department of Leadership and Innovation, Arizona State University

"Principals passionate about closing achievement gaps and ensuring all students achieve to their fullest potential need to read this book. Getting to know the whole student and where they are is key to ensuring students succeed and grow. This book connects the ideas of intelligence and mindsets as they relate to learning and provides advice that principals can believe and follow!" —**Dan Lamboley**, principal, Parkside Junior High School, Normal Unit #5, Normal, IL

"After delving into the in-depth research of *Brain Science for Principals*, I realized my principal colleagues and I have focused ourselves as instructional leaders with a fixed mindset instead of more effective learning leaders or as effective growth leaders. Lyman and her colleagues have done an outstanding job clearly outlining through extensive research what effective educational leaders need to know about neuroscience." —**Randy Simmons**, principal, Peoria Notre Dame High School, Peoria, IL

"Accountability for student growth is at the forefront of every conversation. We are in an age where student growth is the focus of politicians, administration, teachers, parents, and students. *Brain Science for Principals* offers insight into brain research that supports environments that can cultivate learning. I found the book easy to read and helpful in understanding the impact of brain science on education. The format of the book allows for reflection, which leads to implementation of ideas to create a school culture for addressing the needs of the whole child." —**Elizabeth Zilkowski**, principal, Charter Oak Primary School, Peoria School District 150

"Understanding how the brain, intelligence, and emotional control change as children develop is a useful and important skill for educators, not only because of the consequences for learning, but also to help promote equity in schooling. Imagining that the brain can be developed, nurtured, and grown presents a shifted paradigm for principals who make decisions about student learning, disciplinary consequences, and physical activity. Any principal committed to social justice, including learning, would be well served by reading this book with the teachers in the building and exploring the implications for the way we 'do schooling.'" —**Charol Shakeshaft**, PhD, professor of educational leadership, Virginia Commonwealth University

Brain Science for Principals

What School Leaders Need to Know

Edited by Linda L. Lyman

ROWMAN & LITTLEFIELD
Lanham • Boulder • New York • London

Published by Rowman & Littlefield
A wholly owned subsidiary of The Rowman & Littlefield Publishing Group, Inc.
4501 Forbes Boulevard, Suite 200, Lanham, Maryland 20706
www.rowman.com

Unit A, Whitacre Mews, 26-34 Stannary Street, London SE11 4AB

Copyright © 2016 by Linda L. Lyman

All rights reserved. No part of this book may be reproduced in any form or by any electronic or mechanical means, including information storage and retrieval systems, without written permission from the publisher, except by a reviewer who may quote passages in a review.

British Library Cataloguing in Publication Information Available

Library of Congress Cataloging-in-Publication Data Available

ISBN 978-1-4758-2431-5 (cloth : alk. paper)
ISBN 978-1-4758-2432-2 (pbk : alk. paper)
ISBN 978-1-4758-2433-9 (electronic)

∞™ The paper used in this publication meets the minimum requirements of American National Standard for Information Sciences—Permanence of Paper for Printed Library Materials, ANSI/NISO Z39.48-1992.

Printed in the United States of America

Contents

List of Tables and Figures ... ix

Preface ... xi
    Linda L. Lyman

Acknowledgments ... xiii

Introduction ... 1
    Linda L. Lyman

Section I: Learning

1. How Can Learning Be Enhanced? ... 9
    Linda L. Lyman

2. How Does Neuroplasticity Change Belief in Fixed Intelligence? ... 15
    Matthew K. Heid

3. How Does Metacognition Enhance Learning? ... 21
    Jennifer McCoy

4. How Does Being Bilingual Benefit a Learner's Brain? ... 27
    Patricia M. Valente

5. How Does Multitasking Affect Learning? ... 31
    Matthew K. Heid

Section II: The Fit Brain

6. How Does Sleep Build Brain Health? ... 39
    Stacie M. France

7. How Do School Breakfast and Lunch Programs Support Learning? ... 45
    Brian M. Swanson

8	How Does Exercise Enhance Learning? Brian M. Swanson	49
9	How Does Movement in the Classroom Benefit Learning? Abigail Larrison	53
10	How Can Memory Be Enhanced? Linda L. Lyman	59

Section III: The Emotional Connection

11	Why Is a Positive Learning Environment So Important? Jennifer McCoy	67
12	How Do Trauma and Chronic Stress Affect the Brain? Stacie M. France	73
13	How Can Stress Be Recognized and Reduced? Jamie L. Hartrich	79
14	How Do the Arts Nurture and Connect Emotions? Patricia M. Valente	85

Section IV: The Brain on School

15	How Can Mindset Make Someone Smarter? Matthew K. Heid	93
16	How Can Knowing about Brain Science Improve Reading? Patricia M. Valente	99
17	How Can Knowing about Brain Science Improve Math? Jamie L. Hartrich	105
18	How Can Principals Support Teacher Success with ELLs? Patricia M. Valente	109

Section V: Ages and Stages of the Brain

19	How Can Principals Help Elementary Learners? Jamie L. Hartrich	117
20	How Can Principals Help Middle Schoolers Learn? Stacie M. France	123
21	How Can Principals Help High Schoolers Learn? Jennifer McCoy	129

Section VI: Inside the Brain of a Principal

22	How Do Principals Maintain Mindfulness in Challenging Times? Christine Paxson	137
23	How Can Principals Support Environments That Cultivate Learning? Christine Paxson	141

24 How Can Brain Science Inform Cultural Processes? *Christine Paxson*	147
Conclusion *Linda L. Lyman*	151
References	155
About the Authors	163
About the Editor *Linda L. Lyman*	167
About the Consulting Editor *Abigail Larrison*	169

List of Tables and Figures

TABLES

Table 6.1	Recommended Sleep Guidelines	40
Table 12.1	Types and Examples of Stress	74
Table 13.1	Stress Management Skills and Exercises	82–83
Table C.1	Composite Ranking in Descending Order of Importance of Neuroscience Topics to Effective Instructional Leadership (see conclusion)	152

FIGURES

Figure 6.1	Brain Parts Related to Memory Functions	41
Figure 14.1	Relationship of Arts Training and Cognitive Ability	86
Figure 16.1	Brain Systems and Pathways Connected with Reading	100
Figure 23.1	Questions We Should Ask Ourselves as Leaders	142
Figure 23.2	Keeping a Balance with Technology	144
Figure 23.3	This is what work/life balance should look like.	145

Preface

Linda L. Lyman

"We think in the service of emotional goals."

—Mary Helen Immordino-Yang

This book has grown out of my twenty-year interest in educational neuroscience findings and their implications for leadership of learning in schools. Neuroplasticity of the brain is today the most widely accepted conclusion of neuroscience research. Around as a theory since the mid-1800s and heavily researched during the 1990s, neuroplasticity is a term used to explain how the brain is malleable and changes throughout life. Neuroplasticity is redefining the meaning of intelligence. It is no longer acceptable for educators to continue to view intelligence as fixed at birth.

Holding a fixed-at-birth perspective about intelligence is a form of deficit thinking that limits the learning potential of all students. The fixed mindset belief about intelligence has been overturned, and a new reality requires educational leaders who can take schools and teachers to what is now a limitless learning frontier. Neurogenesis and neurodiversity as factors in learning are also opening up thinking and expanding horizons. Recent findings from educational neuroscience can help erase the edges of inequality experienced by those marginalized in schools and society.

The book was designed and written as a final project by seven master's students enrolled in a Principal Preparation Program Cohort class at Illinois State University in Fall 2014. The course catalog description reads succinctly: "Course provides exploration of leadership applications of educational neuroscience to enhance learning capacities from early childhood through adulthood." When I created the course titled Leadership for Stages of Mind, I had not originally foreseen the final product to be a book.

In surveying materials available to use in the course, I found a book about educational neuroscience and learning addressed to college students (Doyle and Zakrajsek 2013). I found a second book specifically addressed to teachers (Wilson and Conyers 2013). But I did not find any books about neuroscience focused on the interests and needs of principals expected to function as learning leaders. Thus, the book emerged as a culminating project requiring *real* learning that would be a *real* challenge and by filling a gap could make a *real* difference.

The class members accepted the challenge to determine questions that principals might have about educational applications of neuroscience, to divide up the questions, to do research, and to write short book chapters about what they learned. As the instructor, I agreed to serve as editor and seek a publisher. Working from course topics, over the first half of the semester the class members sat around a table brainstorming questions for the book, eventually creating a mind map of sticky notes containing twenty-four questions. They collaborated on a Google .doc to do further planning, and then work on the chapters began.

The knowledge base of educational neuroscience reinforces that emotion and cognition are both indeed intertwined. We know that the learning environment matters and that caring leadership can enhance learning. We know that learning about how their brains work can enhance learning for all students. We know that a growth mindset makes a difference to learning.

We need principals who can lead teachers into full understanding of the complexity of learning and the brain. What we now know about learning and the brain is enough to make a world of difference. The time has come to include what we now know about learning and the brain in the education and professional development of future and practicing principals. This book was written to give principals and future school leaders a place to begin.

Acknowledgments

The chapter authors—Stacie M. France, Jamie L. Hartrich, Matthew M. Heid, Jennifer McCoy, Christine Paxson, Brian M. Swanson, and Patricia M. Valente—wish to acknowledge the Educational Administration and Foundations Department faculty and staff of Illinois State University for their consistent encouragement and unyielding support during the writing of this book and throughout our degree-seeking journey. We offer special recognition to Dr. Linda L. Lyman, who believed in our ability to author a book before we believed in ourselves. The success of our journey would not have been possible without the invaluable guidance, cooperation, and time offered by our school principals, colleagues, and students. We are particularly grateful to our family members and friends for unwavering love, for partnership, and for serving as our cornerstones.

As the book's editor, I gratefully acknowledge the support of Illinois State University colleagues and staff in the Educational Administration and Foundations Department during the writing of this book. Department Chair Lenford Sutton fully supported my commitment to this project. Erika Hunt, senior policy analyst for the Center for the Study of Education Policy, offered visionary encouragement for bringing educational neuroscience findings into the new principal preparation program. I am most grateful to the scholars and practitioners who reviewed early versions of the book and offered suggestions. I thank chapter authors Stacie France and Jennifer McCoy for undertaking extra editorial responsibilities that moved the manuscript along. I particularly want to thank former graduate assistant Sruthi Singireddy, who facilitated my 2015 national study of beliefs and attitudes about including educational neuroscience findings in principal preparation programs. Data from that study are reported in the conclusion. I am beyond grateful to Dr. Abigail Larrison, Self-Design Graduate Institute, for providing invaluable input as consulting editor during the final stages of finishing the manuscript. With a PhD in neuroscience and an EdD in educational leadership, she sharpened the focus on how educators can better align schooling with the learning needs of the brain. I am forever grateful to the pioneering cohort of students who took the risks, found the time, and said yes to co-creating this book. Finally, I thank my beloved husband, Dave Weiman. His unfailing support and partnership added joy to the months of writing and editing, and he continues to bring me "a song of love and a rose in the wintertime."

Introduction

Linda L. Lyman

> "Learning is a complicated practice."
>
> —Terry Doyle and Todd Zakrajsek

A comprehensive understanding of recent educational neuroscience findings about learning and the brain can contribute to a principal's ability to be a growth-oriented *learning* leader. Neuroscientifically literate principals have the potential to level the learning field through application of educational neuroscience findings. Principals can and are using the newest information about learning and the brain to help teachers transform classrooms and to help schools to address the way students actually learn.

"A new understanding of the brain is increasingly being linked to increases in student achievement in the elementary grades" (Schachter 2012), but outcomes are also evident at other levels. For the most part, preservice teachers are not getting exposure to educational neuroscience information from their teacher education programs. Teachers who have been in the classroom for a while may not have kept up with these new developments in the study of learning. Therefore, it falls to the principal to recognize whether faculty members are holding outdated conceptions of intelligence, learning, and memory.

In the words of principal Allison Harris (2014), from Smithfield Elementary School in the Charlotte-Mecklenburg School District, recent research findings can prompt change:

> The most exciting of the recent neurological discoveries is undoubtedly the concept of neuroplasticity. Because it proves that the brain can be permanently changed in relation to specific, well-planned experiences, neuroplasticity provides great hope for teachers. Knowing that thoughtfully planned, individualized learning experiences will result in brain cell growth gives teachers a sense of urgency and compels them to view teaching and learning through an entirely new lens.

The shape of minds and lives will change as the field of educational leadership continues moving in the direction of incorporating educational neuroscience findings into schools. New dimensions of knowing and opportunity will open for students, especially those marginalized by current teaching practices, policies, and pervasive deficit thinking. Principals must be prepared to help teachers realize when their understanding of learning is outdated. The most commonly accepted neuroscience finding is the neuroplasticity of the brain. That reality changes our understanding of intelligence.

This introduction has several purposes. The first is to introduce examples of insights about learning and the brain that can transform classrooms and schools. The second purpose is to sketch the development of the collaborative multidisciplinary and international academic field of educational neuroscience that emerged at the end of the twentieth century. The final purpose of the introduction is to present an overview of the book and its chapters.

WHAT IS LEARNING?

The phrase *instructional leader* suggests a focus on teaching, or the instructional process. The phrase *learning leader* implies focus on the learning that occurs in the brains of both teachers and students. Emphasis matters. How, in fact, is learning defined? Do we define it in terms of what is remembered, or does learning include what we have forgotten? If learning is the goal, then what is the role of memory, or what is required of memory?

In the following paragraph, psychology professor Louis Cozolino's (2013) explanation of learning focuses on neurons:

> Learning is believed to occur through changes in the connectivity among neurons in response to stimulation. Repeated firings of two adjacent neurons results in metabolic changes in both cells, resulting in an increased efficiency of their joint activation. In this process, called long-term potentiation (LTP) . . . excitation between cells is prolonged, allowing them to become synchronized. . . . When these connections are made, neurons build more bridges between them. (28–29)

University professors Terry Doyle and Todd Zakrajsek (2013) take a similar approach, offering what they call a new definition of learning:

> What does it mean to say you have learned something? Neuroscience researchers have shown that when you learn something new, there is a physical change in your brain . . . and when you learn something new, some of your brain cells establish connections with other brain cells to form new networks of cells, which represent the new learning that has taken place. (6)

Benedict Carey (2014), science writer for the *New York Times*, introduced an encompassing theory of learning called the meaning maintenance model. The gist of this model is that when feeling lost, "the brain will kick into high gear, trying to find or make meaning, looking for patterns, some way out of its bind—some path back to the campsite" (217). He continued, "If the learner is motivated at all, he or she is now mentally poised to find the way home. Being lost is not necessarily the end of the line, then. Just as often, it's a beginning" (218).

James Zull (2011), professor of biology, biochemistry, and cognitive science, also worked from a journey metaphor to describe how a brain becomes a mind:

> Picture a newborn child with a brain ready to learn. This is where the journey begins. Exquisitely organized for learning, this brain is destined for change as the baby grows into a child and eventually an adult. . . . The change is so dramatic that we need a new word to define it. We call it *mind*. (10)

Zull (2011) finished this line of thought with a metaphorical observation about the source of lifelong learning:

By chance, by personal engagement, and by individual meaning, our brain begins as nascent mind and travels along a path that has no apparent end, but rather leads simply to unexplored territory. Our natural mind takes over, and learning goes on throughout our lives. It is not an end but a process. And it is "our ancient and natural strength." (23)

CONTEMPORARY HISTORICAL CONTEXT OF EDUCATIONAL NEUROSCIENCE

Introduce students of any age to metacognition, to how their brains work, and their learning will increase. Teach them that intelligence is not fixed, that the brain changes every day in response to experience and effort. Then, by teaching them all that has been learned in the past decade about productive study strategies, they can become more successful students. Opportunities to learn about educational neuroscience exist at the state, national, and international levels.

National conferences for principals at the elementary and secondary levels (NAESP and NASSP), as well as those for superintendents (AASA) and educators from all fields and levels (ASCD), are offering conference sessions and strands focused on neuroscience. The American Educational Research Association (AERA) has a Brain, Neurosciences, and Education Special Interest Group (SIG) formed in 1988. To give just one example from the state level, in 2013 the Vermont Higher Education Collaborative offered a Summer Institute Leadership strand titled "Using Principles of Neuroscience to Lead Schools in the 21st Century."

In 1999, *Learning & the Brain* was founded to meet a perceived unmet need in the educational community for neuroscientists and educators to explore new research on the brain and learning and its implications for education. Since then, its conferences and summer institutes have brought together cutting-edge neuroscience and educational research from the researchers themselves to educators, clinicians, counselors, speech-language, and special education professionals to improve their practice. Research centers and labs at major universities, as well as professional organizations, have joined forces as co-sponsors.

In 2008, experts from six countries formally established a new academic discipline called Mind, Brain, and Education (MBE) science (Tokuhama-Espinosa 2010). A panel of thirty-nine experts and the use of a Delphi survey led to an agreement about the shape of the field. Although there were differences of opinion, "the Delphi panel did achieve its primary goal of identifying basic standards in the emerging field" (3). The group was unified in wanting the discipline to be an independent academic field that should not be associated with the term brain-based learning, "which they felt was a label associated with unscholarly research and commercial claims" (3).

According to Tracy Tokuhama-Espinosa's history (2011), "MBE science began as a cross-disciplinary venture between cognitive neuroscience and developmental psychology, but then it reached further beyond these parameters to integrate education via educational psychology and educational neuroscience" (4). Of further interest has been the attempt of MBE members to identify teaching concepts.

These teaching concepts were organized "on a continuum from 'what is well-established' to 'what is probably so' to 'what is intelligent speculation' to 'what is a misconception or neuromyth,'" based on evidence in MBE science (Tokuhama-Espinosa 2010, 3). Just as a developing brain goes through periods of pruning unneeded neurons, the field of educational neuroscience is still in the process of pruning or discrediting neuromyths, those earlier generalizations that represent misrepresentations or exaggerations of data.

The International Mind, Brain, and Education Society (IMBES) publishes a journal and also holds annual conferences. There is agreement that at least three disciplines are involved: mind represents the lens of cognitive neuroscience, brain biology is the focus of neuroscience, and education includes educators and the lens of pedagogy. The conversation among the three fields is contributing to a deeper understanding of learning.

According Tokuhama-Espinosa (2011), included in the field are studies related to specific skills and abilities, or domains (e.g., reading or math). Some disciplines are focused on cognition as a whole (e.g., theories of intelligence). She wrote:

> Additionally, there are three broad categories of studies related to the biological aspect of learning that are essential to an understanding of MBE science: studies on neurogenesis, plasticity, and the mind-body connection (which includes studies on sleep, exercise, and nutrition, and the impact of each on learning). (114–15)

OVERVIEW OF THE BOOK

This book is structured by questions considered important for principals to be able to answer. The questions are organized into sections focused on six overarching topics. Each chapter ends with three questions for reflection. Although the chapters unfold in a logical order, they do not need to be read in order; each chapter is designed to stand alone. Some concepts are addressed in more than one chapter. This guidebook was written to give a busy principal an introductory quick source of information about recent educational neuroscience findings about learning and the brain.

Section I—Learning

Chapter 1 examines how learning is defined, contrasts various theories of learning, presents surprising insights into study techniques, and concludes with practical steps for a principal whose goal is leading learning. Chapter 2 explains how the concept of neuroplasticity has redefined intelligence from an unchanging fixed entity bestowed at birth to a capacity that grows and changes throughout a lifetime in interaction with experiences.

Chapter 3 considers how teaching metacognition to students of all ages will improve their school performance and change their brains. Chapter 4 presents a comprehensive look at how being bilingual benefits a learner's brain. Chapter 5 explores the myth of multitasking, whether it improves learning and why so many people think it does in spite of the evidence to the contrary.

Section II—The Fit Brain

Chapter 6 establishes that sleep is critical for brain health and learning. Chapter 7 describes how school breakfast and lunch programs support learning by mitigating the all too prevalent realities of food insecurity and hunger. Chapter 8 describes the brain benefits of exercise. Chapter 9 explains and illustrates how incorporating movement into the classroom benefits learning. Chapter 10 responds to the relationship between learning and memory, and reports on tested approaches to retrieving and retaining memories.

Section III—The Emotional Connection

Having established a biological background for learning and its enhancement in the previous sections, the authors turn to how and why emotional well-being is critical to learning. Chapter 11 establishes why a positive learning environment is *everything* to students' developing brains. Chapter 12 details the destructive effects on the brain of trauma and chronic stress such as poverty. Successful intervention programs to promote wellness are described, including neurocounseling. Chapter 13 focuses on strategies for recognizing and reducing stress. Chapter 14 illustrates how the arts are uniquely suited to enhance the growth of cognitive, emotional, and psychomotor pathways and interconnections in support of learning.

Section IV—The Brain on School

In this section, the focus is on how teaching strategies anchored in neuroscience enhance learning. Chapter 15 argues for teaching a growth mindset to all students. Chapter 16 considers how knowing about brain science can improve reading. Chapter 17 elaborates strategies for improving math. Chapter 18 includes information about how principals can support teacher success with English Language Learners, a rapidly growing population.

Section V—Ages and Stages of the Brain

These three chapters look specifically at how principals can help students of different ages and stages of development learn. Chapter 19 explains how elementary learners are motivated by curiosity and developing the ability to pay attention. Also emphasized are memory strategies and benefits of collaboration. Chapter 20 pinpoints the uniqueness of the middle school mind, caught between two developmental levels, with an overdeveloped amygdala stimulating emotional responses and an undeveloped prefrontal cortex unable to predictably calm emotion through reason. Middle schoolers respond to well-designed group work and collaboration.

Chapter 21 features the biological basis for the risky, impulsive behavior of teenagers and their particular vulnerability to anxiety, pessimism, and stress. The mismatch of the overdeveloped amygdala and the undeveloped prefrontal cortex is even greater for them than for middle schoolers. For high schoolers positive relationships with teachers can help provide emotional stability and a safe place in the face of cognitive overload and stress.

Section VI—Inside the Brain of a Principal

The final three chapters address critical leadership questions, offering information and reflective frameworks for principals regardless of their school levels. Chapter 22 explores mindfulness as a way of paying attention and a capacity important for leaders in today's complex immediate response environments. Chapter 23 introduces NeuroLeadership, an interdisciplinary subfield with researchers who explore the neural basis of leadership and management practices. The chapter introduces the relationship between NeuroLeadership and emotional intelligence. Chapter 24 focuses on leadership that builds positive cultural processes. Creating emotional resonance is offered as a way of leading, grounded in the domains of emotional intelligence: self- and social awareness, and self- and relationship management.

Conclusion

The conclusion re-emphasizes the need for principals to understand the effects and implications of recent educational neuroscience findings about learning and the brain on leading. The chapter features a report on a national survey completed in 2015 to ascertain existing attitudes and beliefs in the field of educational leadership about the significance of educational neuroscience. What can neuroscience teach principals and school leaders about *leadership of learning*?

A FOUNDATION FOR SOCIAL JUSTICE

A faculty committed to teaching, informed by educational neuroscience findings about learning, builds a foundation for social justice that can create a world of difference in a school. In 2012, principal Lynn Brown shared with *District Administration* magazine writer Ron Schachter that training teachers in both the biology and psychology of the brain has made a difference to learners at the Jacob Shapiro Brain-Based Instruction Laboratory School, a charter school in Oshkosh, Wisconsin. For example, Brown shared, "While 38 percent of the students at Shapiro School started as special education students, that rate had dropped to 25 percent by the time they were fifth graders." Brown explained that "the programs we have based on neuroscience have made a difference."

Students of all ages are benefiting from having neuroscientifically literate teachers who have a growth mindset and who design lessons to take advantage of brain neuroplasticity and maximize student potential. Many more students would benefit if more principals were neuroscientifically literate, able to lead teachers into fuller understanding of the complexity of learning and the brain.

Principals are in a position to bring teachers the professional learning and information they need to become more fully successful with all students. Pervasive deficit thinking about the learning potential of some students will not stand up to the influence of the developing knowledge about the brain and learning. Neuroplasticity, neurogenesis, and neurodiversity offer a new path. This book is offered as a guide for the journey.

I
LEARNING

1

How Can Learning Be Enhanced?

Linda L. Lyman

> "All human behavior and learning, including feeling, thinking, creating, remembering and deciding, originate in the brain."
>
> —Mary Helen Immordino-Yang

This chapter presents practical techniques and strategies anyone of any age can use to learn more easily. The science of learning as a whole focuses on the brain as it is shaped and modified by experience. Brains are not disembodied but work in service of the whole. There is important interplay between the two. Because it is embodied, happening in your brain, all thought is physical. Learning something new causes a physical change in the brain because with learning some of your brain cells establish connections with other cells through synapses, and together these brain cells form a new network of cells that did not exist before. This new network represents the new learning.

Most contemporary definitions of learning acknowledge that through learning the brain is physically changed, a process involving chemicals, electricity, thoughts, and emotions, as neurons fire and wire together. This ever-changing nature of the brain is a feature of its neuroplasticity. Neuroplasticity is a term used to explain how the brain is malleable and changes throughout our lives. Neuroplasticity of the brain as a theory has been around since the mid-1800s. Today, it is the most widely accepted conclusion of neuroscience research. Because of the neuroplasticity of the brain, intelligence is not fixed at birth but can grow and change at any age through interaction with experiences.

Emotion also is central to how our brains learn. In fact, one neuroscientist describes the brain as an organ of emotion. What does that mean in the classroom? Immordino-Yang (2011) wrote: "Put simply, what affective neuroscience is revealing is that the mind is influenced by an interdependency of the body and brain; both the body and brain are involved, therefore, in learning" (99). Said another way, "Children's bodies, brains, and minds are meaningful partners in learning" (101). This intertwining of emotion within our thinking brains helps explain why the brain hangs on most tightly to memories involving the experience of strong emotions.

Conceptualizing the journey from brain to mind, Zull (2011) wrote that "the ultimate outcome of the journey is to understand our own understanding" (15). He identifies the region of the limbic cortex known as the "anterior cingulate" as implicated in self-awareness, as the region that "makes connections between brain areas involved in cognition, and other areas involved in emotion" (256). He identifies metacognition as the link that ties everything together. Zull articulates that metacognition is something we do for ourselves and therefore is a conscious process, a thread that leads to decisions resulting in the joy of learning.

LEARNING IS NOT LINEAR

Educators have in the past believed that becoming educated was like ascending a staircase. Schools have been structured by this conceptual model. According to the theory, we learn in a linear progression as we advance from one grade to the next, from one year to the next. But in fact, cognitive scientists have shown that learning is not such a clear process. There is an ebb and flow as alternative ways of thinking and new approaches develop, regress, and redevelop.

Other theories of learning are being introduced as the stairstep or ladder model loses dominance. "Overlapping waves" is what Robert Siegler, a professor of cognitive psychology at Carnegie Mellon University, calls his theory of intellectual development initially proposed in 1996. Rather than a development proceeding from level 1 to level 2, the stairstep model as it were, Siegler saw instead how different "knowings" ebbed and flowed as new approaches created an alternation of old and new understandings in a child's mind. A student may demonstrate advanced knowing of something one month, and then that regresses and falls back, and another interest takes over. Siegler's image of learning is a series of surging and receding waves. His research demonstrates how this overlapping waves model applies to learners of all ages.

Yet another important model was framed and developed by Kurt Fischer, recently retired professor of education at the Harvard Graduate School of Education, who was one of the founders of Mind, Brain, and Education (MBE). He called his model a "Constructive Web of Development," believing that the staircase model never did capture the way cognitive change or learning actually worked.

Fischer's model clarifies how new skills emerge marked by a cluster of discontinuities that feature reorganizations and new capacities. It is not regular like a spider's web. Examples of such discontinuities can be found in speech, reading, and arithmetic skills. Sometimes, strands of development intersect each other and are coordinated, like when spelling and sound come together in learning to read. Other times, strands split, like when addition and multiplication are understood as separate operations.

TECHNIQUES AND STRATEGIES TO STRENGTHEN LEARNING

Within the past several decades, neuroscience researchers and cognitive psychologists have uncovered a variety of study techniques that deepen learning. Benedict Carey, *New York Times* science writer, made a study of learning and found "techniques that remain largely unknown outside scientific circles" (2014, xiii). Much of what is being discovered absolutely goes against what we have been taught about learning.

For example, whereas educators for years have asked parents to provide students a quiet spot dedicated to studying and doing homework, new research suggests that in fact the brain works more effectively if a person studies in a variety of places and has a variety of study routines and rituals. Furthermore, it is not necessary to use earplugs or a headset to block out noise and sit diligently in one spot.

Moving around is, in fact, good for learning. Breaks are particularly important in a study session because without breaks each new body of information will function as "interference" in the important processes that transfer information into memory. Interference of new information can effectively block the transfer of previously studied material by demanding the system to continuously engage in attending to new and perhaps unrelated content.

Memory science has discovered that effective learning is not about consistency in study habits. Studying at the same time of day and in the same place does not contribute to attention or engagement from brains that are wired to pay attention to novelty. Quiet is not necessary because the context of studying affects memory, and so music particularly may aid memory in fact. It appears that "the background music weaves itself subconsciously into the fabric of stored memory" (Carey 2014, 51). Then, when a student is taking a test, the information associated with music is easier to retrieve or recall. Studies have revealed that having *something* going on in an environment where a person studies is better than having nothing going on.

Another surprising finding is that it is *not* a good idea to devote a lengthy block of time to repetitively practicing what one is trying to learn, like a particular musical scale, for example, or long division. The brain prefers more variety and will pick up patterns and learn more quickly if several kinds of musical passages are included in the practice session and there are breaks, diversions, and periods for reflection.

The same is true for studying math. Mixing up types of math problems promotes better results than repeated drilling on the problem of the day, as featured typically in homework. This is because the brain may habituate to a drill that shuts down higher learning centers. Just think of how boredom plays against interest and engagement. However, for creating an efficient or speeded process, drilling is not a bad approach. Studying needs something to keep it fun, like the power of gaming. The point is that learning is multidimensional, and the goals of learning and practice should be considered when teachers assign work.

Even concentration does not work like we thought it did. "Concentration may, in fact, include any number of breaks, diversions, and random thoughts" (Carey 2014, 217). Breaking up study time—called "distributed learning," the "spacing effect," or "interleaving"—is one of the oldest and most reliable strategies of memory science. For example, an hour of study divided into three twenty-minute sessions over three to five days, rather than an hour of study on a single day, will result in longer retention.

Breaking up studying is particularly important when homework is from several classes. Moving from studying about one topic to another without a break for reflection will lower the quality of learning associated with the first topic because of the phenomenon called "interference" mentioned earlier.

Thinking of the school day, this interference reality has implications for scheduling of, in particular, middle and high school classes. The interference phenomenon encourages administrators to consider programs of integrated curriculum, as students will be primed for learning novel concepts in a new discipline as long as they relate to what they were taught in their previous class. Integrated curriculum across disciplines is perhaps the best way to encourage deep conceptual learning that is stored in long-term memory rather than superficial memorization of facts that have no context and degrade quickly (Drake and Burns 2004).

Carey (2014) also has written that interruptions are our friend when the goal is learning because interruption, the supposed enemy of learning, sets up the opportunity for percolation and further reflection. Percolation takes the learning broader and deeper. Recall that learning reflects cellular changes occurring in the brain. These changes happen through protein synthesis, and that takes time. Carey advocates for leaving things just a bit unfinished when working on a large project of any kind.

Interrupting oneself a little early on purpose to make time for percolation is a good thing. Having a paper or project unfinished causes the mind to be sensitive to relevant information in one's environment, and the thinking evolves as more knowledge accumulates. Therefore, quitting work on something does not put it to sleep, but rather keeps it awake. Percolation can benefit many types of complex creative projects, not just writing projects.

In terms of changing classroom dogma, one of the more significant findings is the discovery of the Default Mode Network (DMN) (Raichle et al. 2001). For decades, teachers and administrators have been focused on keeping students *on task*. If students are not doing something, then they are not participating. They are not learning. The recent research on the DMN shows that even when persons are *not* engaged in any specific tasks, a precise network of brain regions are observed to be active.

This network includes the frontal lobe and is easy to identify in resting state functional MRIs. Hence, the brain is engaged in critical thinking and problem solving even when it appears the student is simply day dreaming. It is that state of restful brain activity that neuroscientists now report as critical to creative processes and problem solving. Percolation happens during activation of the DMN. This is when the neural networks of new learning are allowed to take form. Whatever causes it, however it is described, we all benefit from downtime.

The more information principals have about learning and the brain, the more they can contribute to transforming learning in classrooms and schools. Development of schools focused on learning for all requires teachers to become neuroscientifically literate. The information is out there, with new findings accumulating daily. Principals have a role to play in developing these neuroscience literacies.

HOW CAN PRINCIPALS ENHANCE LEARNING?

Much has been written about the responsibility of a principal for instructional leadership. Principals are understood to play an important role in whether a school does or does not meet the standardized testing requirements and state learning standards omnipresent in schools across the country. Learning is measured by standardized high stakes testing. Scores must meet certain minimum accountability standards, or the principal may be out of a job.

The principal is expected to be able to lead learning improvement through a focus on data analysis to identify patterns and causes of weakness in the student scores. The responsibility typically rests with the principal and school improvement team to identify strategies to remedy the learning gaps revealed by the scores. These remedies can be arrived at in a building or district-wide. Providing appropriate professional development for the teachers and building a culture and climate for learning are considered essential skills for a principal.

Clearly, however, instructional leadership needs to be about more than data analysis. Should a principal focus on being an *instructional* leader or a *learning* leader? What difference does the terminology make? Each phrase sets up a different metaphor, with *instructional leadership* suggesting an external focus on the data, teaching process, and the teachers. In contrast, a *learning leader* models learning, values relationships, and attends to the learning needs of everyone who comes in the school door. A principal with a deep understanding of learning and how it happens has a better chance of enhancing learning for everyone involved in a school community.

CONCLUSION

The following list gives practical suggestions for how a *learning leader* can incorporate recent findings about learning and the brain into the culture and climate of a school community:

- Hold periodic "learning conversations" with faculty individually and in groups to share new information about learning and the brain.
- Ensure that the curriculum includes metacognition and time for teaching students age-appropriate strategies for how to learn.
- Encourage faculty to build reflection time into classes to minimize interference, known to lower the odds of learning transferring into memory processes.
- Use informal classroom observations to look for how new information about learning and the brain is being incorporated.
- Work with policy makers to protect scheduled time for physical education and recess and later start times that honor the needs of teenagers for more sleep.
- Develop a school climate that reduces student stress and anxiety, whether caused by bullying or information overload associated with high stakes testing.
- Communicate new information about learning and the brain with the school community through newsletters and websites and at open house events.

The most commonly accepted neuroscience finding is the neuroplasticity of the brain. Neuroplasticity changes our understanding of intelligence. To enhance learning, educate teachers about neuroplasticity, meaning that intelligence is not fixed at birth. Introduce students of any age to metacognition and teach them how their brains work. Teach them that the brain changes every day in response to experience and effort. Teach them what has been learned in the past decade about productive study strategies so they can become successful students and experience the joy of learning.

QUESTIONS FOR REFLECTION

1. Does it matter how the principal defines learning?
2. What was the most surprising information about learning strategies in the chapter?
3. In what ways could you assess whether you have a neuroscientifically literate faculty?

2

How Does Neuroplasticity Change Belief in Fixed Intelligence?

Matthew K. Heid

> "Many educators hold on to the traditional mindset that a child's level of intelligence is what he is born with and therefore his intelligence quotient is relatively stagnant throughout life."
>
> —Allison Plunket Harris

French psychologist Alfred Binet developed the first IQ test in 1905. It was a short thirty-question test related to everyday problems of life. American psychologist Lewis Terman coined the term "intelligence quotient," but not until 1916. Among the general public, the belief is that a person with a high IQ is smart. Among educators, a high IQ in a student is also regarded as a sign of high ability, and therefore such students are offered different paths, options, and enrichment than children who do not have higher than average IQ scores.

Intelligence as a score did not exist until Terman decided to use Binet's test. It was in this 1916 Stanford-Binet revision that the intelligence quotient, or "IQ," was first used as a score to quantify intellectual functioning so individuals could be compared. The validity of the concept of a fixed IQ has continued to function culturally in support of the traditional view of intelligence typically reflected in explicit theories of intelligence.

Is intelligence biological or cultural? Beth Hatt (2011) argues that "judgments about intelligence or smartness are based on implicit cultural understandings of the term" as they operate in school settings (2). She states that "smartness or implicit intelligence is something done to others as social positioning" (2). Hatt's belief is that "all those involved in the institution of schooling help to shape who we think we are, who others think we are, and who we think we can become" (2). Definitions of intelligence can come from many points of view.

NEUROSCIENCE VIEWS OF INTELLIGENCE

According to Donna Wilson and Marcus Conyers (2013), "Teaching students that intelligence is dynamic, malleable, and changeable is the first step toward developing the belief that they can get smarter through hard work and persistent effort" (75). They define brain plasticity, which they also call neural plasticity, as "the ability of neurons (cells) in the brain and synapses (the structures that allow neurons to pass information to one another) to change throughout the life span" (46). This ability means that the brain is from birth always adapting and creating new neuropathways between neurons. It means that intelligence is not fixed at birth.

Neurogenesis is considered part of the larger process of neuroplasticity. Research by Eriksson et al. (1998) established that neurogenesis, or the origin of new cells including neurons, does happen in the adult human brain. Some evidence exists that hippocampal adult neurogenesis is important for learning and memory. According to Gregory Elder, Rita De Gasperi, and Miguel Gama Sosa (2006), "It is now accepted that neurogenesis occurs in two brain regions in adult mammals, namely the hippocampus and olfactory bulb. In both regions new neurons arise from a resident population of neural progenitor cells that are maintained throughout adult life" (931).

The neuroscientists' discoveries supporting neuroplasticity and neurogenesis require educators at all levels to reconsider conceptualizations of intelligence. The IQ score approach to understanding intelligence is an entity view of intelligence, the view that intelligence is largely genetic, fixed at birth, and unchanging throughout a person's life.

OTHER CONCEPTIONS OF INTELLIGENCE

A comprehensive discussion of possible conceptions of intelligence is beyond the scope of this chapter. Examples of approaches, however, include that of Robert Sternberg, Linda Jarvin, and Elena Grigorenko (2009), who divided the theories on intelligence into two major categories. The first category includes "single-faceted," or general theories. The second category includes "multifaceted" theories. Additionally, Raymond Cattell (1971) and John Horn (1968) speculated that fluid intelligence and crystallized intelligence were two subfactors that made up a general factor.

Sternberg (1999) developed a triarchic theory highlighting metacognitive, performance, and knowledge-acquisition components. These were regarded as leading to analytical, creative, and practical aspects of intelligence. He articulated a conception called successful intelligence, which features "the ability to achieve success in life, given one's personal standards, within one's sociocultural context" (292–93). He and his colleagues developed the WICS model to help teachers implement his ideas in the classroom. WICS stands for wisdom, intelligence, creativity synthesized—and emphasized memory and analytical skills.

Carol Dweck (1999), whose work with mindset is well known, offers yet another perspective, distinguishing between incremental and entity views of intelligence. From the incremental perspective, intelligence is changeable or malleable. In contrast, from the entity view intelligence is seen as something fixed and stable. Typically, those with an entity view have a fixed mindset about people's ability to improve their intellectual capacity. On the other hand, those with an incremental view tend to have a growth mindset regarding the possibility of a person's getting smarter.

WHY DO TEACHERS' VIEWS OF INTELLIGENCE MATTER?

How teachers view the subject of malleable intelligence has consequences for what students will learn, for their academic performance. Teachers' beliefs about intelligence affect students. Dweck (2008) contends that teachers with a fixed mindset tend to create a different atmosphere in the classroom than those with an incremental view. Those working from a fixed mindset view have been found to be more judgmental while those holding a growth mindset focus on nurturing what they regard as the developing intelligence of their students. Unfortunately, about a quarter of preservice and in-service teachers believe that intelligence is fixed according to research by Brett Jones, Lauren Bryant, Jennifer Snyder, and David Malone (2012). This leads to the categorization and discounting of the intelligence of learners who display variability from the norm.

Studying implicit theories of intelligence held by preservice and in-service teachers, Jones et al. (2012) found that students have more control over their own developing intelligence if teachers have an incremental view of intelligence than if teachers have an entity view. The students see that their intelligence can be increased through studying and learning. In general an incremental view of intelligence has been linked to higher student achievement plus an increase in factors related to students' motivation—they devote more effort, try harder, and demonstrate more concentration.

In exploring how preservice teachers defined intelligence, Jones et al. (2012) found the following themes emerging:

- Achievement . . . is characteristic of an intelligent person
- Declarative knowledge . . . possesses in-depth factual knowledge
- Procedural skills . . . functions well in social situations
- Self-regulation . . . higher level of self-discipline or metacognition
- Cognitive processes . . . higher levels of thinking and/or learning capacities
- Motivation . . . higher levels of general motivation plus an inquisitive nature
- Personal characteristics . . . included open-mindedness toward differing points of view and humility (92–95)

Of the 270 persons who took the Jones et al. survey, 77.9 percent reported an incremental view of intelligence. However, "about a quarter of the preservice [total of 237] and inservice [total of 33] teachers in this study believed that intelligence is fixed" (98). "One implication of this study is that teacher educators need to examine how they convey beliefs about intelligence to their preservice teachers" (98). Jones et al. (2012) also shared the finding that "other researchers have reported that teachers' judgements of students' intelligence can impact the students' views of intelligence" (90).

SUPPORT TEACHERS WITH A GROWTH MINDSET

Wilson and Conyers (2013) posit that "no matter how we define intelligence, the evidence indicates that education affects it" (83). Teachers' beliefs about the malleability of intelligence affect students' beliefs. Principals are encouraged to try to discern the implicit theories of intelligence held by teachers when observing in their classrooms. Classrooms of teachers with growth mindsets tend to display these characteristics:

- High standards
- A nurturing environment
- Guidance for deliberate practice
- Praise for effort

- Focus on mastery goals
- The use of formative assessments
- An emphasis on thinking skills, such as memory skills, analytical or critical thinking skills, creative skills, and practical skills, and wisdom-based skills (84–89)

The ability of any individual to get smarter is supported by the neuroplasticity of the brain. Potential and intelligence are not fixed at birth—genetics play a role but do not determine what a person can accomplish. According to Wilson and Conyers (2013), "the concept of experience-dependent synaptogenesis suggests that people learn and develop based on their environment and the experiences they have in life" (90). Intelligence is changed and shaped throughout life.

How can principals use the information about neuroplasticity of the brain to improve instruction and the educational processes for students? Specifically, research supports that students benefit from learning that intelligence is not fixed (Chen 2014). A principal can organize professional learning experiences for faculty around recent findings of educational neuroscience, the malleability of the brain, and incremental theories of intelligence.

Principals can organize focus groups to examine effects on learning of the growth mindset and fixed mindset. Principals can encourage teachers to develop and teach from a growth mindset. Principals can insist that teachers know about neuroplasticity and its implications for intelligence and learning. Whatever their ages, students need to be taught how their brains learn.

CONCLUSION

Wilson and Conyers (2013) state that "the concept of flexibility in intelligence allows teachers, parents, and policymakers to focus on improvement with greater confidence in the outcome" (75). Many people know the term "IQ" and believe it to be a number that represents how smart a person is. Most people have little understanding of what the term IQ actually means or where it originated. The misconception is the widespread belief that IQ stands for intelligence and is something a person is born with, that it is fixed and cannot be changed. This misconception is harmful and can limit the abilities and potential of students of all ages.

Christina Hinton, Kurt Fischer, and Catharine Glennon (2012) write that "arguably the most important insight for education is that the brain is highly adaptive, a property called plasticity" (3). Plasticity describes the ability of neurons (cells) in the brain, and synapses to change. Synapses are structures that allow neurons to pass information to one another through electrochemical processes. New synapses are created through a process called *synaptogenesis*, and elimination of unneeded synapses occurs through a process called *pruning*.

Experiences the students have over time through the mastery of a whole variety of experiences result in their brains continuously learning and adapting to the environment. We now have evidence from neuroscience of the brain's neuroplasticity and capacity for neurogenesis throughout the life span. Evidence of neuroplasticity and neurogenesis requires us to give up the outdated idea that intelligence is fixed at birth. Principals are in a leadership position that makes it possible for them to bring knowledge of recent neuroscience findings about the brain and learning to the teachers with whom they work.

The belief that intelligence is fixed at birth has been used in the classroom to label students and limit their success as learners. Instead of using teaching strategies based on the concept of a fixed IQ and other misconceptions about learning, teachers who experience the most success are those who focus their teaching on research-based strategies that incorporate knowledge about neuroplasticity, neurogenesis, emotion and stress, the role of attention, executive function, movement and learning, arts and learning, sleep and learning, and creativity. Intelligence is a multifaceted, complex concept.

QUESTIONS FOR REFLECTION

1. Are there myths and misconceptions in your school about what an IQ score means?
2. Do different theories of intelligence engender different kinds of learning?
3. What professional development activities could educate a teaching staff about the marginalizing effects of believing a student's IQ score indicates a fixed intelligence?

3

How Does Metacognition Enhance Learning?

Jennifer McCoy

"Knowing yourself is the beginning of all wisdom."

—Aristotle

Metacognition works with developing students' self-awareness and self-reliance, practices that may not be central components of traditional curriculum. Metacognition is a process of becoming aware of one's own brain processes as they occur during thinking. It is often defined as thinking about thinking, or knowing about knowing. Through using metacognitive strategies a person's thinking strengths can be focused on projects and lead to positive outcomes. Metacognition gives students a map to their own minds. It opens the door to a world of self-directed and self-regulated learning opportunities.

COGNITION AND METACOGNITION

Donna Wilson and Marcus Conyers (2013) include teaching metacognition as one of their five big ideas for effective teaching using brain science. Specifically, they hold up "the need for explicit instruction on metacognition, or thinking about one's thinking with the aim of enhancing learning" (2). Metacognition, in fact, is one of the most well-researched approaches for improving school performance of students of any age and helping them come closer to achieving their potential.

How do we encourage students to think about their thinking? This process can be taught and integrated into curriculum. More reflective students may do it naturally, but even they will benefit from being taught strategies of self-reflection and self-awareness during their learning. Teaching metacognition can be integrated into typical content lessons.

Begin, for example, with the learning of a particular math problem. After students spend time enough to solve the problem, the teacher asks each student to describe how he or she reached the answer. This might be done through peer sharing or by going through the steps of how the problem was solved as a group, and labeling what the students just accomplished.

This process encourages students to think about their thinking and problem-solving processes. Teaching metacognition can begin at any age using age-appropriate learning tasks.

Wilson and Conyers (2013) assert that "*explicit* instruction on metacognitive strategies supports the process of learning and can be applied across *content* areas and in students' lives outside of school" (111). With younger students, some educators talk about metacognition as "teaching the students 'to drive their brains'" (111). Young students who learn to drive their brains can grow into teenagers who are developing executive function ahead of schedule, at least some of the time. Cognitive strategies from any field can be taught, and then students can reflect on how well they are using the strategies. Developing metacognitive ability is an example of a virtuous circle.

Judy Willis (2010), a former practicing neurologist who made a career change and became a middle school math teacher, thought she would be able to save more brains as a teacher than as a neurologist. She defines cognition as "the mental process by which we become aware of our surroundings and use that information to solve problems and make sense out of the world" (176). Cognition is something that develops as our brains and minds grow and learn. However, metacognition is a more complex concept that results in a layer of thought surrounding cognition. Learning how to be metacognitive happens through a process of reflecting on how something was learned and becoming aware of the cognitive strategies used in that process.

Correspondingly, if cognition deals with a person's thinking, then metacognition is reflecting on that thinking and describing the process. Willis (2010) described metacognition as "knowledge about one's own information processing and strategies that influence one's learning. After a lesson or an assessment, prompting students to reflect on the successful learning strategies that they used can help reinforce effective strategies and optimize future learning" (178). Willis makes time for teaching metacognition in her classroom practices. For example, after receiving the results of a test or project assessment, the students with her guidance take the time to analyze what and *why* they did well, and what and *how* they could have done better.

LEARNING CHANGES THE BRAIN

If students are to be lifelong learners, then as they develop they must accept the importance of understanding their own brains. One approach effective in encouraging students to understand the importance of their active engagement and self-direction is sharing with students the knowledge that learning literally changes the brain. While the growth mindset (the idea that intelligence can increase through focus and practice) is beginning to make inroads into schools, the fixed mindset (the idea that intelligence is determined by genetics) is still alive and well in public education and current culture.

Students frequently excuse poor academic performance by shrugging, *I'm not good in math* or *I don't like to read*. Parents do not aid development of a growth mindset when they sigh at their child's report card, *Oh, I was never good in that subject, so he must get it from me*. A parent's sharing of such a negative personal belief may limit a student's engagement in critical academic content.

Very young students tend to have smaller differences among their wide-ranging interests, while older students specialize and restrict their areas of interest. As John Hattie and Gregory Yates (2014) put it, "Particularly when children move into adolescence they tend to move from 'being good at everything' to backing themselves in fewer domains" (218). The problem with this domain preference develops when students begin to think that one content is *not their thing* or that they *can't do* that subject.

In the words of Richard Bach (1977), author of *Illusions*, "Argue for your limitations and sure enough they're yours" (100). True enough, when students tell themselves they *can't* and excuse this defeatist behavior because something is *not their area*, they miss opportunities to exercise their brains' plasticity, to master new or complex material, and literally to change their brains.

We know that intelligence is one of a number of other cognitive capacities that are dependent on nurture (environment) and nature (genes); they are not entirely predetermined at birth. In other words, skill, mastery, and ability come from experience as much as biological maturation. Aristotle said, "We are what we repeatedly do. Excellence, then is not an act, but a habit."

A growth mindset involves practicing metacognition. Through practice and habit, students can increase their capacity to learn by becoming aware of their own personal learning process (Jensen and Snider 2013). Teachers who understand this and teach students explicitly about their brains and ability to acquire new skills have the power to make the greatest impact on student learning.

Wilson and Conyers (2013) elaborated, "The concept of flexibility in intelligence allows teachers, parents, and policymakers to focus on improvement with greater confidence in the outcome, especially in the case of low-achieving students" (72). But without students' awareness of their own learning, of how their own brains can change, this point is lost. According to Alden Blodget (2013), "Meaningful learning (the sort of learning educators hope to foster) results from an active effort to understand, an effort that promotes the growth of increasingly efficient webs of neural connections among different regions of the brain" (3).

STUDENT ATTITUDE

Metacognition grows from a student's attitude and understanding of self. It does not just benefit students who have a poor sense of their ability or sense of self. Students who have perceived themselves as being smart or have been told throughout their lives that they are gifted or intelligent are equally at risk of failing to look at how their behaviors or actions toward learning impact their performance.

Talented students often hit the proverbial brick wall when they are faced for the first time with a serious academic challenge (Hattie and Yates 2014). However, when students are taught that their learning is not based on some intrinsic worth but rather on their continued effort, then they will show even greater persistence and motivation to work at difficult tasks. As this work ethic and associated study habits develop, students begin to demonstrate greater confidence and growth in academics.

METACOGNITIVE STRATEGIES

In addition to explicitly teaching students how their brains work, as well as facilitating their self-awareness as learners, the following research-supported strategies for supporting metacognition are best practices (see Doyle and Zakrajsek 2013; Hattie and Yates 2014; Jensen and Snider 2013; Wilson and Conyers 2013):

1. *Labeling*: Avoid labeling a student as "smart" or dismissing struggles as "not the student's area"; labels or classifications promote a fixed mindset and may cause students to back away from the effort metacognition requires.

2. *Managing emotions*: Students should be taught reflection about their emotional responses so they recognize when reactive negative emotions are interfering with their ability to receive new concepts. Reactive negative emotions can also block access to prior knowledge. Teachers can model emotion management skills through *think alouds* and coaching of students who are struggling.

3. *Connecting*: Making connections deliberately by connecting new concepts to students' previous knowledge is a key method educators can teach students for increasing understanding and retention. Making connections is a metacognitive strategy that can improve students' engagement and effort. Learning can be increased by engaging students in interacting with new material through a variety of learning modes—speaking, listening, writing, reading, drama, and the expressive arts. In fact, Doyle and Zakrajsek (2013) assert that "the stronger the connections in [the student's] brain become, the more likely the new learning will become a more permanent memory" (7).

4. *Distributing practice and taking breaks*: Cramming produces the illusion of learning, but does not contribute to long-term memory. Because today's bloated information-based curricula imposes a form of cramming, today's students need to be taught how to use distributed practice over time to solidify their learning and mastery of skills. When encountering new concepts, they need to understand the importance of breaks—processing or reflection time—for their brains to consolidate and understand new material. A class activity can feature keeping time and then allowing an equal time for processing and reflection.

5. *Think/pair/share*: The purpose of this metacognitive technique is to have students think about their responses to a prompt and then share them with a partner. They can share with a partner first before speaking about them to the entire class. A variation would be having each student report on the other student's response in the pair instead of their own.

6. *What's the story?*: The purpose of this metacognitive technique is to connect themes or ideas to a meaningful story that can help students remember something. The students create a story using the content of a particular lesson, with each student adding one sentence featuring a key concept or element to the story.

7. *Organizing*: Investing in teaching students organizational skills can pay enormous dividends—for both the students and teachers. Not only are these skills that translate across the curriculum and throughout a student's lifetime, but also being organized reduces the stress that can interfere with a student's ability to comprehend and retain new information. Becoming organized is a critical step in self-regulation and self-directed learning.

FEEDBACK AND MODELING

Teachers play a vital role in aiding students' metacognition. Key components for increasing students' awareness of their learning processes are feedback and modeling. Because learning is a risky endeavor for students, they need the reassurance that helpful feedback provides. Feedback tells students that the risk is worthy of their effort and gives them the tools to shape their understanding and hone their skills. Brain development and learning are not linear processes. Learners may take a long time to learn a complex task and then master several other tasks very quickly.

Skillful teachers use think alouds to model thinking immediately in the classroom during steps in the learning process. This practice gives students methods for connecting to the skills needed to master the content. Additionally, by providing adequate, specific feedback with steps for improvement, educators can scaffold complex materials for students of all ability levels. Teachers also encourage metacognition by framing mistakes or failures as opportunities for learning. Taking time to talk through and help students understand their mistakes by modeling metacognition will result in deeper, long-term memory and skill development, whatever the content.

CONCLUSION

Teaching students about their brains and metacognition can yield powerful results at any level. Having students take control of their own learning, reflect on possible learning processes, and become actively engaged in decisions for *how* they learn is the ultimate goal of any good instructor. Metacognition and a growth mindset go together in promoting self-engagement in productive, joyful learning. However, students may remain *stuck* if their mindsets are fixed. If they believe they can't, they won't. Thankfully, it takes only one teacher to make a positive difference in students' lives—a teacher who believes in his or her students and models metacognition and a growth mindset.

QUESTIONS FOR REFLECTION

1. How can teachers incorporate metacognitive instruction within their content instruction?
2. In what ways can learning metacognitive processes influence student (and teacher) motivation?
3. How would you recognize the effects of teaching metacognition in a classroom?

4

How Does Being Bilingual Benefit a Learner's Brain?

Patricia M. Valente

"If you talk to a man in a language he understands, that goes to his head. If you talk to him in his language, that goes to his heart."

—Nelson Mandela

Many languages are spoken throughout the world. People have the natural ability to understand and learn the language that is spoken around them, so every person knows and speaks at least one language. If each person has the natural ability to learn language, why not learn two languages? It is a misconception to believe that speaking two languages could be a handicap.

Being bilingual offers the learner a greater understanding in two different languages, along with flexibility in thinking. It not only improves the understanding of the native language, but also makes other cultures more easily accessible. Researchers now believe that when people learn another language, they develop cognitive advantages that improve their attention, self-control, and ability to deal with conflicting information.

MYTH AND MISCONCEPTION

A common myth and misconception is the belief that children exposed to two languages will be confused. According to John Benson (2013), "A lot of people, even pediatricians, used to be worried that speaking more than one language to a child was going to confuse them, but we know now more than ever that's not the case, and in fact, there may be advantages of bilingualism." Children exposed to bilingual input typically learn two languages without obvious difficulties. Researchers now believe that when people learn another language, they develop cognitive advantages that improve their executive function, attention, working memory, self-control, and ability to deal with conflicting information.

ENHANCED DEVELOPMENT OF EXECUTIVE FUNCTION

More specifically, bilingual children experience greater development in what is called executive control, or the executive function. The executive control system is a network in the brain's frontal lobe that is busy focusing the mind's attention to the language being used while screening out the second language not being used. The network is a kind of traffic control system that helps organize and regulate thinking (Freemark and Smith 2014).

The constant juggling of two languages means that the brain must have a way to control a person's access or interference of either language at a given time. This is an important skill in communication. A bilingual person must maintain a balance between the two languages by relying on the executive function. The bilingual person uses the executive function to monitor the two language systems, which are always active and competing for attention. This constant practice strengthens the executive function and changes the brain regions associated with it (Marian and Shook 2012).

ATTENTION

Studies on the processes of attention used by children have established that the attentional brain network is related to self-regulation of cognition and emotion. It is involved in attending to high-level skills, including making word associations. For instance, during the act of attending to one language while suppressing related responses in another language, the executive attentional network is the one more likely to be active, according to Laura-Ann Petitto (2008), a developmental cognitive neuroscientist.

Improved attention to detail comes from bilinguals' ability to focus on information about the new language while reducing the interference from the language they already know. The strong capacity to focus their attention might be what leads to better academic performance in some children who grow up bilingual or attend language immersion programs.

Petitto et al. (2012) found in her research on the brain and language that developing bilinguals' healthy language processing creates an advantage. She compared younger and older bilinguals with younger and older monolingual babies. The finding of the study was that older bilingual babies' resilient neural and behavioral sensitivity to phonetic contrasts, found in other (foreign) languages, was stronger at a time when monolingual babies could no longer make such discriminations.

Petitto et al. (2012) wrote, "The bilingual baby's sustained (more open, longer) phonetic discrimination capacities are good. It can afford the young bilingual child increased phonological and language awareness, meta-language and pragmatic awareness, as well as cognitive benefits—and, more upstream, stronger reading, language, and cognitive advantages" (142). She found no evidence of neural "disruption"—no developmental brain atypicality—when a baby is exposed to two languages as opposed to one. No evidence has been found that being "monolingual" is the "normal" state of affairs for the human brain and that being exposed to two languages, in effect, presents a kind of neural trauma to the developing bilingual child.

OFFICIAL SEAL OF BILITERACY

Several states as well as national professional organizations are beginning to draft recommendations for a special recognition, a seal of biliteracy, to be included on high school diplomas and transcripts for graduates who demonstrate fluency in two or more languages. Professional organizations involved are the American Council on the Teaching of Foreign Languages, the National Council of State Supervisors for Languages, the National Association for Bilingual

Education, and the TESOL International Association, which is spearheading the effort. The movement is already under way in some states.

Educators working to bring about the seal of biliteracy believe the seal could give students an advantage upon high school graduation. It could open doors for college scholarships, internships, and jobs that require proficiency in a language other than English. States already offering such a seal or recognition are California, Illinois, Louisiana, Minnesota, New Mexico, New York, Texas, and Washington.

Proposals for seals of biliteracy are also under consideration in Indiana, Massachusetts, Nevada, Rhode Island, Utah, and Virginia. Jacque Van Houten, the president of the American Council on the Teaching of Foreign Language, endorsed the concept: "The seal serves to certify attainment of biliteracy for students, employers and universities. It is a statement of accomplishment that helps to signal evidence of a student's readiness for career and college, and for engagement as a global citizen" (Mitchell 2015).

CONCLUSION

The cognitive, neural, and social advantages observed in bilingual people reveal how bilingualism shapes the activity and architecture of the brain. In general, bilinguals tend to enjoy far sharper cognitive skills, keeping the brain constantly active. Their ability to strike a balance and switch between two languages eases the transition between various tasks. When presented with distractions, bilinguals can maneuver them skillfully while displaying a more heightened concentration on their assignments than the monolinguals.

Speaking more than one language increases mental flexibility, or neuroplasticity. People fluent in one or more languages seem to express a much higher degree of environmental awareness. This means that the ability to process and "monitor" external stimuli sharpens alongside the verbal abilities. Because bilinguals must toggle between languages, bilinguals' brains become fine-tuned to pick up on subtleties and patterns both on and off the page. Being bilingual is a benefit to the brain.

QUESTIONS FOR REFLECTION

1. How do you think being bilingual will benefit your students in the twenty-first century?
2. What are the benefits for your school in having bilingual students?
3. In what ways can the school show appreciation and learn from its bilingual population?

5

How Does Multitasking Affect Learning?

Matthew K. Heid

"Simply put: your brain is not wired to do multiple things at once."

—Sandra Bond Chapman

Educational neuroscience is changing the understanding of learning and teaching practices around the globe. Imaging technology has contributed to the rapid increase of knowledge about the brain and learning by making it possible to look inside brains of living people of all ages. Neuroimaging technologies developed in the past twenty-five years have revealed much that was previously hidden.

These technologies began in the 1970s with the CAT (computerized axial tomography) scan and now include EEG (electroencephalogram), PET (positron emission tomography), and fMRI (functional magnetic resonance imaging). These scanning methods show brain function noninvasively by measuring blood flow in the brain and how that blood flow changes as activity in an area of the brain increases or decreases.

Until imaging technology made it possible to see what was happening in a brain during the process of learning, much of what was believed about the brain was not verifiable and fell into the category of neuromyth. "*Neuromyths* are typically born of a partial fact or a single study and are overgeneralizations about the brain—or in some cases, outright misinterpretations of data" (Tokuhama-Espinosa 2011, 90). For example, in the early 1900s, experiments in France with removing part of the brain tissue from a variety of animals were followed by observations that the animals seemed to function without total, intact brains.

These observations apparently were the foundation for the neuromyth that we use only 10 percent of our brains. Myths about the brain typically arise when something plausible is presented as speculative but interpreted as fact or distorted. So if a small part of a brain lobe is sufficient for an animal to function, humans probably use only 10 percent of their brains, someone thought, and another neuromyth was born. Older neuromyths still hang on, and newer ones continue to develop. Tracey Tokuhama-Espinosa (2011) developed a list of twenty-nine common neuromyths and misconceptions about learning, such as the belief that "everything important about the brain is determined by the age of three" (82). Another example from the list is "learning can be isolated from the social/emotional content" (82), a clearly untrue statement.

DEFINING MULTITASKING

Christine Rosen (2008) defines multitasking from a historical perspective: "Used for decades to describe the parallel processing abilities of computers, multitasking is now shorthand for the human attempt to do simultaneously as many things as possible, as quickly as possible, preferably marshalling the power of as many technologies as possible" (105). Hallowell calls multitasking a "mythical activity in which people believe they can perform two or more tasks simultaneously" (Rosen 2008, 106). Hattie and Yates (2014) call it a "widely held fallacy" (107).

John Hattie and Gregory Yates (2014) offer an array of definitions for multitasking. They explain that the term can be applied to any of the following:

- The brain accomplishing two or more activities simultaneously
- Accomplishing multiple goals within a single time period through switching between tasks
- Focusing on one primary goal but periodically allowing other tasks or secondary goals to assume priority
- Consciously dividing your time attending to several essentially nondemanding tasks, such as monitoring e-mail, watching the oven, and listening to a radio program (187–88)

Multitasking is a myth that has arisen in tandem with the proliferation of computers and communication/media technology. Multitasking is thought to be a skill and is commonly defined as doing two or more activities simultaneously. However, if the tasks are at a high level cognitively or involve learning and thinking, most psychologists would agree that what has been termed multitasking is actually task shifting or task switching occurring when the brain switches attention between one task and another very rapidly. Performing an action already learned that has established automaticity, like walking for example, is something that can be done simultaneously with other tasks.

THE MYTH OF MULTITASKING

Although not technically a neuromyth, multitasking has taken on mythic proportions in many lives. Media multitasking is experienced as a way to extend the mind's ability to be productive. Sometimes it functions as entertainment, a relief from boredom. Sometimes it is simply a way to keep up with the onerous burdens of the world of work. Although multitasking has become second nature, habitual multitaskers may resist recognizing that the effects on learning are not always positive. With any level of switching between demanding tasks, performance lapses will occur.

Multitasking seems a necessity in today's society, where information is constantly being transmitted and processed, but closer consideration reveals that it comes with lapses in performance that are called "switching costs." In the words of Hattie and Yates (2014), "To put it bluntly: when it comes to actual learning situations, *multitasking does not exist*. Students ought to be discouraged from believing they have the capacity to do two things at once, if one such activity involves any form of learning" (188). John Medina (2014) states with equal certainty, "Multitasking, when it comes to paying attention, is a myth. The brain naturally focuses on concepts sequentially, one at a time" (115). The attentional ability required for learning demands focus.

An array of studies reported by Rosen (2008) in *The Myth of Multitasking* present other negative aspects or consequences of the practice. Studies conducted by psychologist René Marois at Vanderbilt University have used fMRI imaging to demonstrate how the brain handles multiple tasks. He found evidence of a "response selection bottleneck" (Rosen 2008, 107), which occurs when the brain is forced to respond to several stimuli at the same time, as happens with multitasking. These bottlenecks result in lost time and less learning. Studies conducted by Russell Poldrack, a psychology professor at UCLA, found that "multitasking adversely affects how you learn. Even if you learn while multitasking, that learning is less flexible and more specialized, so you cannot retrieve the information as easily" (Rosen 2008, 107).

Jordan Grafman, chief of cognitive neuroscience at the National Institute of Neurological Disorders and Stroke (part of the National Institutes of Health), used fMRI scans "to determine that when people engage in 'task-switching'—that is, multi-tasking behavior—the flow of blood increases to a region of the frontal cortex called Brodmann area 10" (Rosen 2008, 107), one of the last parts of the brain to evolve. Psychologist David Meyer at the University of Michigan has found that "multitasking contributes to the release of stress hormones and adrenaline, which can cause long-term health problems if not controlled, and contributes to the loss of short term memory" (Rosen 2008, 107).

It may seem like a student is multitasking while listening to the teacher and texting a best friend, but in reality, the brain is switching back and forth from texting to listening very rapidly. Students say they can handle it all—instant messaging, iTunes, cell phone calls, e-mail, and texts to name a few—while doing their homework. Yet the more activities one tries to handle in a task-shifting mode, the more difficult it becomes. Additionally the more cognitively demanding one of the tasks is, the more difficult it becomes to effectively complete either or any task.

ISSUES OF MULTITASKING PRACTICES IN SCHOOLS

In spite of proof to the contrary, people today still claim that they are experts at the practice of multitasking. Although they may become much faster at task shifting than adults are, students are still not able to do two things at once either. Studies have established that members of the younger generations are indeed better at task shifting with simple tasks than are members of older generations, but members of all generations share difficulty when the tasks being attempted simultaneously are cognitively challenging.

An additional consideration involved with multitasking in educational settings is the evidence that the overloading caused can lead to decreased memory and executive function when carried to an extreme. For young people, multitasking may come with a cognitive cost. With too much pressure the desired learning may never become part of long-term memory (Medina 2014; Rosen 2008). Sandra Chapman (2013) asserts that "multitasking is bad for your brain and actually weakens your higher-order thinking capacity" (74). She lists as major costs of multitasking both the lost time and "a buildup of cortisol, the stress hormone that decreases our memory and contributes to increased brain cell death" (75).

This chapter is focused on an important question for principals to consider: *How does multitasking affect learning?* The answer is that doing too much task shifting can have a negative impact on learning, attention, and memory. Multitasking negatively changes the way one learns and lowers the ability to stay focused on one task. Additionally, trying to multitask can create stress in the form of information overload, which has other side effects. According to Medina's (2014) *Brain Rules*, it takes twice as long to complete a task when trying to multitask, plus mistakes are much more likely. With schools today demanding that all students achieve at high levels, task shifting while trying to learn can be a major hindrance to the learning process.

Problems with learning originate at any age with multitasking if we ignore what is known about how information becomes retained in long-term memory. For new learning to arrive in long-term memory, we must process information for enough time and without interference from other incoming information. New learning is not facilitated by jumping back and forth between sources and tasks. At best, we quickly scan for information that will need to be explored in more depth if it is to be retained.

WHY TASK SHIFTING CONTINUES

Zheng Wang and John Tchernev (2012) ask, "Why do people increasingly multitask at high cognitive cost?" Their study suggests that what we call task shifting continues for two reasons.

First, it plays on the emotional aspect of the brain in that the student might enjoy one task and then by association enjoy both tasks more. They give an example of participants who were studying for a test while watching TV: "Their multitasking might lead them to feel satisfied not because they were effective at studying, but rather because the addition of TV made the studying entertaining" (509). To elaborate, "The myth of multitasking actually is partially caused by the misperception of the efficiency of multitasking and by positive feelings associated with the behavior, which is emotionally satisfying but cognitively unproductive" (510).

A second reason task shifting continues is that it becomes habitual in nature: "Our [Wang and Tchernev's] findings show that habitual needs increase media-multitasking and also are gratified by multitasking" (2012, 510). Task shifting also creates a cycle of self-reinforcing needs and gratifications. Hattie and Yates (2014) report that "the laboratory studies with adults indicated that multitasking affects deep learning more dramatically than simple learning, and this is an important factor to emphasize when advising students, and helping them to identify the myths that abound in this area" (191).

CONCLUSION

Educational leaders and teachers need to continue to communicate with students and their families about the negative effects of multitasking on learning. While it may seem enjoyable to be texting while the teacher is talking or to watch television while trying to study, these practices can actually be damaging to the learning process, and certainly learning will not be improved.

Pros and cons of school policies allowing media devices in the classroom need careful consideration. A focused policy could provide a potential remedy for in-school time: allowing students to benefit from technology but also limiting its use when it is not the focus of the learning objective.

QUESTIONS FOR REFLECTION

1. Are the technology policies in the school where you work aligned with the research on multitasking?
2. How can faculty develop the ability to recognize when learning programs and other resources perpetuate neuromyths?
3. How can you educate faculty and staff about the myth of multitasking and the damaging effects it can have on learning?

II
THE FIT BRAIN

6

How Does Sleep Build Brain Health?

Stacie M. France

"I love sleep. My life has the tendency to fall apart when I'm awake, you know?"

—Ernest Hemingway

How many hours of sleep did you get last night? How about the night before? Do you have a sleep schedule, ensuring that you get eight hours nightly? Do you have sleep rules (if you are wondering what sleep rules are, then you probably don't have any!)? Anyone who has been around parents of young children has observed how carefully parents plan the sleep patterns of their infants and toddlers. Why do parents obsess about their infants' sleep patterns? Isn't it because young ones who don't get enough sleep are fussy and no fun to be around? Is the same true about older children and adults?

HOW IMPORTANT IS SLEEP REALLY?

The Centers for Disease Control and Prevention (2013) reports that "insufficient sleep has been linked to the development and management of a number of chronic diseases and conditions, including diabetes, cardiovascular disease, obesity, and depression." This makes getting a good night's sleep look like a pretty serious matter—medically speaking! In an era when maximizing student learning is critical, we must ask ourselves: does sleep affect learning for school-aged children?

The answer is yes. Sleep is important before and after learning. Sleep before learning helps prepare the brain, and sleep after cements the new information. The best way to remember something new learned during the day is to sleep on it overnight. Snoozing strengthens new memories formed throughout the day and links the new memories to earlier ones.

A 2014 survey conducted by the National Sleep Foundation reported that 96 percent of parents indicated that sleep was extremely important or very important for their "child's performance at school." Torkel Klingberg (2013), a professor of cognitive neuroscience at the Stockholm Brain Institute, once heard a teacher say, "Just give me children who've had nine hours' sleep and a proper breakfast every day, and I'll show you that we can raise the mean score on standard assessment tests by 20 percent" (138).

In general, scientific researchers would agree with these wise parents that the proper amount of sleep is critical to learning. Memories become more stable over night during deep sleep, and the brain goes through memories and decides what to keep and what not to keep. Lack of sleep can cut learning ability by as much as 40 percent, according to the National Institutes of Health (2012). Many would agree that sleep is crucial to memory, in particular to the interactive functions of working memory, long-term memory, and attention.

HOW MUCH SLEEP DO WE NEED?

Caring adults do their best to be certain children have school supplies, but it might just be that adequate sleep is the more important preparation for school that children need. If this is true, how much sleep do children need? Information from the National Institutes of Health (2012) in table 6.1 provides sleep guidelines.

WHY IS SLEEP SO IMPORTANT FOR LEARNING?

To answer that question, we must first consider two areas of the brain, the neocortex and the hippocampus. The hippocampus stores new information or short-term memories and has a limited amount of memory storage capacity. The neocortex has a greater amount of memory storage capacity and stores long-term memories. Information stored in the hippocampus is more likely to be lost, whereas information stored in "the neocortex will be more stable and have a greater likelihood, if practiced, of becoming long-term memories" (Doyle and Zakrajsek 2013, 17). Therefore, the neocortex and the hippocampus are intimately involved with learning and sleep. Figure 6.1 indicates these brain parts.

While sleeping, our short-term memories, which are stored in the hippocampus, are moved to long-term memory storage in the neocortex. Remember that the neocortex holds memory in a more stable form that contributes to increased learning. The movement of memories from short-term storage in the hippocampus to long-term storage in the neocortex occurs during sleep.

In fact, the most crucial time for memories to be moved from the hippocampus to the neocortex is during the last two hours of sleep (e.g. from hour 5.5 to 7.5 or hours 7–9) (Maas and Robbins 2011). Therefore, when we reduce our sleep duration, we are decreasing the brain's ability to move memories from short-term storage to long-term storage. This effectively decreases the learning we keep from the prior day.

Table 6.1. Recommended Sleep Guidelines

Years of age	Daily sleep recommendation
0–3	16–18 hours
4–5	11–12 hours
6–12	10 hours minimum
13–19	9–10 hours
Above 20	7–8 hours

Source: Adapted from the National Institutes of Health, http://www.nhlbi.nih.gov/health/health-topics/topics/sdd/howmuch

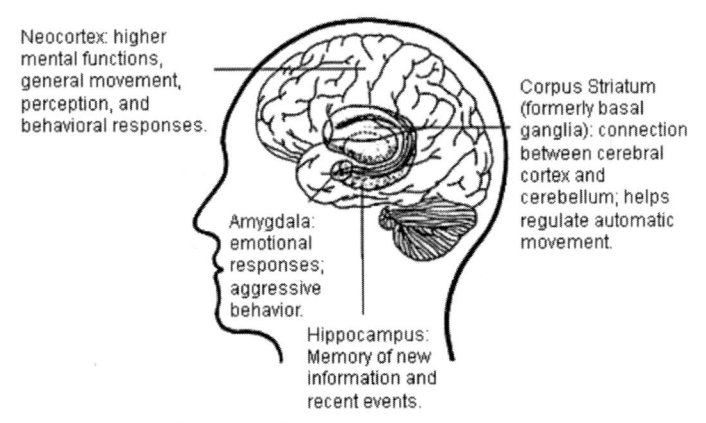

Figure 6.1. Brain Parts Related to Memory Functions

WHAT INTERFERES WITH SLEEP IN SCHOOL-AGED CHILDREN?

A 2014 study conducted by the National Sleep Foundation found that technology in the bedroom is a key factor in whether American adults and children are getting adequate sleep. Technology can be a television, a video game, a smartphone, a laptop, a tablet, an MP3 player, or a radio. A television was the most common bedroom technology. According to the National Sleep Foundation study, "72 percent of children age 6–17 usually have at least one of those five types of devices in their bedroom. 45 percent of these children have at least two of the five types of electronic devices in their bedrooms, including 27 percent who have three or more" (33).

School-aged children whose devices are always turned off during school-night sleeping hours got forty-two minutes more sleep nightly than those whose devices were turned on, and their sleep quality was rated higher. Light emitted by these technologies could partially be to blame for the diminished sleep quality. Light triggers wakefulness in our bodies. Therefore, if these devices must remain on, dimming the light emitted or covering the light could increase sleep quality. If sleep quality is reduced, the brain will not be as efficient in moving the short-term memories stored in the hippocampus to the long-term memory storage of the neocortex.

In the National Sleep Foundation study (2014), 34 percent of parents cited evening activities as interfering with adequate sleep at least once during the week prior to the study. Modern families feel societal pressure to enroll children in a plethora of evening activities. Yet child experts would argue that modern children, especially middle and upper class children, are overbooked and overcommitted in the evenings.

If evening activities are reducing the amount of sleep children get weekly, then those activities are also increasing stress for children and their families. Sleep is crucial to mood regulation. Therefore, modern families must carefully consider whether the benefits of the evening activities outweigh the cost to sleep and therefore learning, as well as the cost to familial and personal harmony.

REMEDIES FOR SLEEP INTERFERENCE

To take the lead, principals can begin by sharing about the importance of sleep with teachers, parents, other people who support student success, and students themselves. Habits, such as sleep patterns and active lifestyles, are not easily altered behavioral patterns. Therefore, repeated offering of the information about sleep is vital to change. Fortunately, principals have many opportunities to communicate with families through newsletters, website updates, open houses, and parent–teacher meetings and during informal conversations. Small signs in hallways or occasional notes in the daily announcements could remind students and staff about the critical nature of sleep to both groups.

SCHOOL START TIMES AND SLEEP PATTERNS OF TEENAGERS

Many school-improvement efforts center on increasing test scores or improving attendance. At the high school level, attention focuses on boosting graduation rates. What if improving student attendance, decreasing student depression, increasing graduation rates, and raising student grades could all happen with one change? Research asserts that aligning school start times to teenagers' circadian rhythms and shifting teenage sleep patterns could have all of the aforementioned benefits (McKibben 2014a).

Of course, school culture and traditions, as well as systems that support schools such as transportation or athletics, may initially balk at this suggestion. But shouldn't current research on what is best for children inform our decisions, not past practice or what is most convenient for adults? With the onset of puberty, hormonal fluctuations cause changes in behavior, which is no secret to anyone who has spent time with a teenager!

Even the sleep pattern changes in teens are caused by hormones. Scientists have discovered that melatonin, the sleep hormone, is released later in teens than in adults and children. In general, adult bodies begin to release melatonin between 9:00 and 10:00 p.m., whereas teenagers' bodies begin to release melatonin between 11:00 p.m. and 12:00 a.m. Therefore, there is a biological reason that teens go to bed later.

If teens are going to get the nine to ten hours of recommended sleep daily, they will awaken later. With the large growth spurts that the bodies of teens go through, the proper amount of rest is critical. As adults who are responsible for understanding and advocating what is best for students, we must consider our school start times in light of teen circadian rhythms. Does your school start time allow for teens to get adequate rest if they follow their natural bedtime inclinations? Probably not, because not many schools or high schools would want to begin at 10:00 a.m., but there are smaller changes that have proved effective.

In the mid-1990s, Edina (located in Minneapolis) and Milwaukee High Schools delayed their start times by over an hour, allowing them to begin at 8:30 and 8:40, respectively. One was predominately white, middle and upper class, whereas the other was highly diverse with a large low-socioeconomic population. Although the student populations were different both schools showed similar benefits. Each experienced higher attendance rates, increased standardized test scores, reduced depression rates, and improved graduation rates. Initially there was opposition to the change, yet after seeing the results both schools still have the later start times today.

Without education about teen circadian rhythms, there will not be policy change. Therefore, a necessary first step is to share information. Are school boards and district office staff, as well as parents, informed or do they just think teens become lazy? As a change agent for "what is best for kids," it is a responsibility of principals to educate for change. Begin by making a list of people or groups to have informal conversations with about teen sleep habits. Let the response to these conversations dictate your next steps. Perhaps you will find an ally, or you may uncover concerns about change. Either result has value. Whatever it is, don't let the response stop you from advocating for students' best interests.

CONCLUSION

Having clearly established the vital nature of sleep to long-term learning and memory formation, we must begin intentionally scheduling sleep for young minds to learn most effectively. If learning is truly a priority, then we must provide school-aged children with the information that sleep is a necessary tool to meet the academic challenges they face in schools.

Principals also must take the lead in advocating for the alignment of high school schedules with teenagers' changed biological clocks. Teenagers especially need more sleep than they are able to get given the typical starting times for high schools. Especially the behavior patterns and learning of teens would benefit from more sleep. In our go-go-go American society, parents, teachers, and other adults must take the lead and guide children and teenagers in understanding that sleep is a cornerstone to learning and academic success.

QUESTIONS FOR REFLECTION

1. Develop a list of sleep patterns that could be implemented in homes of children attending your school.
2. What can you share with families about the importance of sleep for their child's academic success?
3. How could you begin conversations in your district about aligning school start times with the circadian rhythm of teens?

7

How Do School Breakfast and Lunch Programs Support Learning?

Brian M. Swanson

> "If you do not have a healthy, balanced diet and eat before you begin new learning, you are starving your brain of the energy it needs to function properly."
>
> —Terry Doyle and Todd Zakrajsek

When born, an infant's brain weighs approximately a quarter of a pound, whereas the average adult brain weighs around three pounds and is about the size of two fists. Benedict Carey (2014) writes, "The average human brain contains 100 billion neurons, the cells that make up its gray matter. Most of these cells link to thousands of other neurons, forming a universe of intertwining networks that communicate in a ceaseless, silent electrical storm with a storage capacity, in digital terms, of a million gigabytes" (3–4).

By age three, the brain has grown dramatically and produced billions of cells. In their article, Billie Enz and Jill Stamm (2013) posit that "the brain is not a mass of neural cells; instead, it is a highly organized, complex, multifunctional organ. The brain is divided into two hemispheres that are connected by the *corpus callosum*, a band of nerve fibers that carries messages between the left and right hemispheres" (174). It is in the limbic system where "the sensation of hunger and thirst" originate (175).

The brain is, first and foremost, a survival-seeking organ. Quoting Enz and Stamm (2013), "The brain is the most metabolically active organ in the body. Therefore, it is highly dependent on a continuous supply of fuel—blood glucose" (184). The brain is only 1/40th of the body's weight, but its glucose consumption is equal to one-fifth of the body's total consumption (184). When operating normally, the adult brain generates enough electricity to power a twenty-five watt lightbulb.

HUNGER AND FOOD INSECURITY IN LOW-INCOME FAMILIES

School breakfast and lunch programs support learning by filling the nutritional gap for the millions of children who live in low-income families across the United States. The effects of hunger, malnutrition, and the resulting stresses on brain development can result in irreversible brain damage (http://www.30hourfamine.org/2011/11/affect-of-hunger-the-brain/). In 2014, an estimated 14 percent of households in the United States were categorized as food insecure, meaning that they lacked access to enough food for an active, healthy lifestyle for all family members. Very low food security was experienced by 5.6 percent of families.

Programs sponsored by the federal government to combat hunger in school-aged children include the National School Lunch Program, School Breakfast Program, Child and Adult Care Food Program, Summer Food Service Program, Fresh Fruit and Vegetable Program, and After-School Snacks and Suppers. These programs promote child nutrition. A former principal of an early-childhood center in Peoria, Illinois, remembers the reaction when the school he was the principal of began serving breakfast:

> Hinton instituted serving breakfast at Harrison, the first school in the district to do so. One difference he immediately noticed was that fewer students were getting sick at lunch, as many had previously when they had not eaten since the day before. The response of students was so dramatic that at first teachers thought the children were getting too much sugar because they had become so active, he recalled. (Lyman 2000, 67)

Today, numbers of children living in poverty have increased around the country, in both urban and rural areas. Hunger and food insecurity are conditions that accompany increased poverty. Food insecurity is identified as being unable to afford balanced meals, cutting the size of meals because of too little money for food, eating fewer nutritious food choices because of cost, and being hungry because of generally too little money for food. The degree of food insecurity varies from state to state. The typical (median) food-secure household is calculated to have spent 26 percent more for food than the typical food-insecure family of the same size and composition.

When children live in prolonged poverty and hunger, damaging chemicals are released in their brains (http://www.30hourfamine.org/2011/11/affect-of-hunger-the-brain/). Development is delayed at the cognitive, social, and emotional levels. These developmental delays include reading, language, attention, memory, and problem-solving capabilities. Additionally, hunger hinders ability to focus and study. Students are likely to continue to perform poorly if they experienced hunger early in their lives. According to the www.30hourfamine.org website, hunger results in a lower IQ and less developed brain matter. Hunger also affects the decision-making functioning of the brain.

ROLE OF SCHOOLS IN MEETING STUDENTS' NUTRITIONAL NEEDS

The School Breakfast Program (SBP) provides cash assistance to states to operate nonprofit breakfast programs in schools and residential child-care institutions. The Food and Nutrition service administers the SBP at the federal level. State education agencies administer the SBP at the state level, and local school food authorities operate the program in schools. Schools may apply to participate in the SBP at the same time they apply to participate in the National School Lunch Program (NSLP). In 2014 some 7.4 million children in more than 72,000 schools started the school day with food from the SBP.

The NSLP is open to all children enrolled in a participating school, which includes approximately 95 percent of all public schools. During the 2012–2013 school year, 30.7 million children participated. Of that number, on a typical school day, 21.5 million, or 70.5 percent, were receiving free or reduced price lunches. Brains need high-quality nutritious food to have a steady supply of glucose for physical and mental energy. The school breakfast and school lunch programs provide students with quality meals that are necessary to their survival. For some students, the school's breakfast and lunch programs provide their only consistent quality nutrition. Many schools in low-income areas send students who live in low-income families home with backpacks of food for the weekend.

In many low-income areas, increasing poverty is creating areas called *food deserts*, because the grocery stores close and move elsewhere. When this happens, families are left without convenient access to groceries, creating a double burden. Many of the schools are now undertaking extensive feeding programs in low-income areas during the summer break. When planning and creating the nutrition programs in our schools, we must take into account that for too many students these are their only regular meals.

FOOD CHOICES TO SUPPORT LEARNING

The Centers for Disease Control and Prevention (2014a) outlines healthy food recommendations, such as complex carbohydrates, which are often found in fruits, whole grains, and vegetables, for quality nutrition and maximum energy. It recommends avoiding simple carbohydrates, which include sugars and white flour such as doughnuts, white bread, and bagels. In contrast to the longer-lasting nutritional benefits from complex carbohydrates, simple carbohydrates feed the brain for only a short period of time, providing a sugar rush or sugar high.

Besides quality carbohydrates, protein is also an important key in maximizing the brain's energy potential. Quality proteins include eggs, lean meats, and milk. Combining hydration, healthy complex carbohydrates, and quality protein can help students' brains become learning powerhouses. Ensuring that students' brains are prepared to learn is a critical component for principals to monitor and should not be overlooked or underemphasized.

According to the Centers for Disease Control and Prevention (2014a), schools can ensure that the available food and beverage options are healthy and nutritious. Ultimately, this provides students with foods that meet dietary recommendations for fruits, vegetables, whole grains, and nonfat or low-fat dairy products. Schools need to provide all students with opportunities to consume a variety of foods and beverages throughout the school day. A comprehensive approach to nutritional foods will enable all students to learn to their full potential. What a person eats doesn't just affect physical health but contributes to healthy brain functioning as well (Nies 2014).

Water makes up more than two-thirds of the human body. The brain is made up of approximately 80 percent water (Nies 2014). During a night of sleep a person can lose a significant amount of water and upon awakening may be dehydrated. Even mild levels of dehydration can affect the brain's learning performance. Neurons in the brain hold water in tiny balloon-like structures known as vacuoles (Medina 2014). The water is needed for the brain's production of hormones and neurotransmitters, critical components to the communication system of the brain. A person who is dehydrated can ultimately experience fatigue, poor concentration, and reduced cognitive abilities.

If a person is not eating a healthy, balanced diet, then the brain is at risk. In addition to hydration, students' brains require nutritious food for energy to learn. The brain will perform more efficiently and effectively when blood glucose levels can be relatively stable (Medina 2014). With so many food options available, it is also important for schools to serve quality foods that will benefit the brain in learning. A dehydrated and/or hungry brain is one that is not ready to pay attention and learn.

CONCLUSION

It's critical to understand the importance of hydration and properly feeding the brain to prepare for peak learning. School breakfast and lunch programs are keys to a school's ability to guard students' brains from the possible ravages of hunger and food insecurity. In many school districts, when students are not getting the quality foods that are provided by these programs, their capacity to learn is greatly hindered.

Principals play a key role in maintaining school breakfast and lunch programs. Principals support learning by making sure that every student has the opportunity to eat quality foods while at school. Additionally, through outreach to the community for assistance, principals can help minimize the effects of poverty on the children in its most vulnerable families.

QUESTIONS FOR REFLECTION

1. How can a principal ensure that all students are eating breakfast and lunch while at school?
2. How could the school breakfast and lunch programs be revamped to ensure they are providing quality foods?
3. How can a principal involve community members in ensuring that students are not suffering from hunger?

8

How Does Exercise Enhance Learning?

Brian M. Swanson

"Exercise doesn't make you smarter . . . it just makes you normal."

—John Medina

The Centers for Disease Control and Prevention (2014b) recommends that young people from six to seventeen years of age participate in at least sixty minutes of physical activity daily. Physical activity is composed of three types—aerobic, muscular strength, and bone strengthening activities. Aerobic exercise is any activity that elevates an individual's heart rate, such as brisk walking, jogging, or even running. Muscular strengthening activities include weight lifting (age appropriate) or gymnastics. Finally, bone strengthening activities include jumping rope or running.

Donna Wilson and Marcus Conyers (2013) report that "research on the role of physical education in optimizing both body and brain functioning dates back to the 1950s" (Sibley and Etnier, 2003). In fact, Benjamin Sibley and Jennifer Etnier's meta-analysis of forty-four recent studies had multiple relevant findings for policy. They learned that expanding physical education did not decrease academic achievement. They also found much evidence for the positive impact of exercise on learning. These findings suggest that a strong argument can be made for keeping a physical education program.

An illustration of how exercise support from the policy level can show results for learning is a 1999 study from the Naperville Public Schools in Illinois. The school district added aerobic exercise to the junior high curriculum. Results were significant increases on test scores, including tests on which US schools typically rank low. For example, "the eighth grade students in Naperville finished first in the world in science, just ahead of Singapore, and sixth in math, trailing only Singapore, South Korea, Taiwan, Hong Kong, and Japan" as reported by John Ratey (2008, 14). Another positive benefit was a 66 percent decline in behavior problems after the introduction of aerobic activities.

Sibley and Etnier (2003) also found an association between exercise and cognitive gains to be especially strong for the younger participants in the studies they reviewed. The strong relationship between aerobic fitness and academic performance engages students in moving in the direction of developing executive function skills useful for higher-order thinking. At the same time, other researchers found an association with social as well as cognitive development to be a benefit of exercise.

Although the recommendation for sixty minutes of daily physical activity is important for an individual's overall well-being, according to the Centers for Disease Control and Prevention (2014b) only 27.1 percent of students in school participated in daily physical activity, and only 29 percent attended a daily physical education class. In too many districts physical education classes are being eliminated as a way to cut costs and make more time available for learning. This is counterproductive to learning goals, however. According to the Centers for Disease Control and Prevention (2014b), evidence has shown that even low levels of physical activity are beneficial. Any form of physical activity and exercise is better than none at all when it comes to improving students' brains and their learning potential.

HOW DO PHYSICAL ACTIVITIES BUILD THE BRAIN AND ENHANCE LEARNING?

Physical activity and exercise benefit the body but are even more important for building and maintaining a strong and healthy brain. When people typically think of exercise and physical activity, it is easy to name the many benefits exercise has on the body. Physical activity is commonly known to help build muscle, maintain bone structure, reduce the risk of diabetes, reduce cardiovascular disease, and reduce the risk of obesity, to name only a few. Benefits for the brain and learning are equally important.

Harvard psychiatrist John Ratey's (2008) work on exercise and the brain focuses on three ways that exercise may enhance learning: "First, it optimizes your mind-set to improve alertness, attention, and motivation; second, it prepares and encourages nerve cells to bind to one another, which is the cellular basis for logging in new information; and third, it spurs the development of new nerve cells from stem cells in the hippocampus" (53).

Exercise releases a protein called BDNF (brain-derived neurotrophic factor), which keeps brain cells functioning and growing. Some call it the master molecule of the learning process. Discovered by Carl Cotman in 1995, since then thousands of studies have demonstrated the power of BDNF to improve every aspect of the learning process at the cellular level. Greater amounts of BDNF mean "your brain is better able to make the connections between the brain cells (neural networks) that are the physical representation of what you have learned" (Doyle and Zakrajsek 2013, 37). BDNF produced by exercise actually makes learning easier.

Ratey (2008) described BDNF as a fertilizer for the brain and credits it with encouraging neurogenesis—the creation of new cells. According to Medina (2014), "The cells most sensitive to neurogenesis are in the hippocampus, inside the very regions deeply involved in human cognition" (31). Its association with the hippocampus is why a blood volume increase in the dentate gyrus plays a role in memory formation. Other researchers have shown that when the brain is low on BDNF the brain shuts itself off to new information. Exercise also contributes many brain benefits by increasing the production of the neurochemicals serotonin, dopamine, and norepinephrine. These neurochemicals contribute to alertness, attentiveness, and a positive mood (Doyle and Zakrajsek 2013).

The brain cannot go without oxygen for more than five minutes without risking serious and/or permanent brain damage. Blood is constantly being circulated throughout the body all the time. Any tissue in the body without enough blood supply will ultimately starve to death; this includes the brain. The brain needs blood just like every other part of the body, and the more access a brain has to blood and oxygen, the better. In a healthy brain the blood's delivery system can be improved through exercise and physical activity (Nies 2014).

EXERCISE INCREASES CIRCULATION

As a person exercises, blood flow is increased throughout every single tissue in the body. Exercise simulates the blood vessels to create a powerful flow-regulating molecule called nitric oxide (Medina 2014), which results in new blood vessels that penetrate deeper into the body's tissues. As this blood flow is continuously increased, new blood vessels are created by the body, which further improves blood flow.

Ultimately, the more a person exercises, the more tissues can be fed throughout the body and waste can be eliminated from the body. This doesn't just happen only in the brain, but all over the body. Returning to the central question about what exercise does for our brains, the benefit from exercise, simply stated, is more blood in our brains bringing in food (glucose) for both energy and oxygen. All of this helps stimulate protein development, which keeps the neurons in the brain connecting and allows the cells to combine in networks. According to Doyle and Zakrajsek (2013), exercise facilitates communication among brain cells.

Many components contribute to the academic performance and overall achievement of a particular student, such as parents' academic level, socioeconomic status, location, and diet, to name a few. Understanding each of these components and identifying which are the most important for academic achievement can be difficult. With that being said, current research indicates that one common variable for those who think well is *exercise*, exercise that began when they were young children. Physically fit children are able to identify visual stimuli more quickly than those who are not physically fit. Not only are these students able to identify visual stimuli much quicker, they are also able to concentrate longer. There is a relationship between exercise and being mentally alert.

CONCLUSION

By supporting the important role of exercise in learning and ensuring that students exercise daily, principals can ease stress in teachers' work lives and improve student learning. Students with access to exercise during the school day can learn more. Exercise helps students feel better about themselves, have higher self-esteem, and feel less depressed and anxious. With creative leadership, schools and classrooms can help all students meet and exceed the recommendations for daily physical activity, which will contribute to brain health and learning.

Even simple ideas work, such as having students take a break in between classes to do some jumping jacks or just to walk around (Howie, Newman-Norlund, and Pate 2014). Medina (2014) also recommends considering having recess twice a day. Some schools are experimenting with treadmills and bikes in classrooms. The benefits of exercise are countless, but the key argument for exercise in schools is that it supports better academic progress and achievement for students of any age.

Medina (2014) noted studies that indicated increased cognitive abilities for children and adolescent students when exercising. Through exercise, the executive function is strengthened in individuals so they are able to distribute cognitive resources for a particular task, and do so for longer periods of time. Additionally, after activity, children are able to maintain their attention on subjects in school. Studies have also shown that students are less likely to demonstrate disruptive classroom behavior when they're active or have been active.

The information in this chapter reveals how brains benefit from exercise. Moreover, the release of certain chemicals and proteins during exercise causes the brain to be better prepared and equipped to learn. Much evidence supports the importance of exercise for enhancing students' ability to learn. Getting exercise is the best way for people of any age to enhance their own learning.

QUESTIONS FOR REFLECTION

1. What can you do if your school does not require the recommended amount of physical activity?
2. What is the best way to promote physical activity in a school setting?
3. What are ways to incorporate exercise throughout the school day?

9

How Does Movement in the Classroom Benefit Learning?

Abigail Larrison

"The mind is inherently embodied. Thought is mostly unconscious. Abstract concepts are largely metaphorical."

—George Lakoff, *Philosophy in the Flesh*

Teachers often express frustration with students getting out of their seats, running around the room, or getting up to sharpen pencils when they obviously have several sharp pencils in their desk. This behavior disrupts the classroom and can lead to students missing content and even becoming labeled with behavior disorders. Why are students, especially boys, so often unable to sit still? More importantly, we must ask ourselves, why are we demanding students to sit still? What false beliefs do we have about the nature of learning that it is equated with sitting still in a desk for hours on end?

The motor systems of the brain are integral for student learning. These are the first systems to develop and are especially critical in the early grades (Gogtay et al. 2004; see Hannaford 2005). What is less commonly understood is that motor systems are the foundation for attention systems and movement helps to build the frontal networks of the brain that are critical for attention and executive functions. Ironically, the elimination of recess in favor of more academic content by some well-meaning administrators may be contributing to an increase in attention problems and poorer executive functioning.

ACTIVITY-DEPENDENT CONNECTIVITY

A component of neuroplasticity that should be central to a teacher's understanding of the brain is that neuroplasticity itself depends on activity or experience. For motor systems, this means movement. As an analogy, think of the baby who starts to babble before he talks; the babbling is a natural process that occurs because the language systems of the brain are beginning their first stages of development. The parent doesn't have to teach the child to babble. The brain needs stimulation of those regions, and so the behavior occurs. If you stop a child from babbling, these networks do not develop, and the child will not learn to talk. In the same manner, if you stop a child from moving, the critical connections necessary later for higher cognitive control of movement will be blocked, and the students will show problems in controlling their movement, may appear hyperactive, and will have problems with attending to new information.

MOVEMENT, ADHD, AND DYSLEXIA

So why do boys have seemingly more problems staying still? Based on the neuroscience of gender, men have more complex motor systems of the brain, while females have more complex verbal regions. Because of this complexity, they require more stimulation, a greater number of experiences to encourage the neuroplasticity to take place.

Teachers will agree that girls do far better in our elementary education system today. The system is designed for them. They do well learning through listening and reading. Girls like to talk and communicate ideas. All of these activities are helping build the verbal centers of the brain. Boys, on the other hand, need to move to build their motor systems. But our traditional model of teaching doesn't encourage movement. The failure to provide movement reduces the opportunities for activity-dependent neuroplasticity.

The motor system is not just about movement. It begins with the sensory input and is more rightly called the sensorimotor system, or even somatosensorimotor system. The input to the sensorimotor system comes first from the body (i.e., muscles, skin, and joints). As this information enters, it is integrated with visual inputs, which help students become oriented in their bodies in space.

Have you ever seen a student come into the classroom, bump into the desks and walls, and knock over the pencil holder on the desk before finally making it to his seat? Students who have not developed the full connectivity of these bodily senses are not consciously aware of their bodies in space. So when you see a student like this you need to get him moving. But the type of movement such disembodied students require is more than simply sports (although sports can't hurt). The types of activities needed to build the connections with the frontal lobe require awareness and intention.

Movement is connected with our intention. It is directly linked to our willpower and motivation and plays intimately with learning. Sensorimotor inputs from the body go through a central network of the brain, the basal ganglia, critical not only for motor control but also central to motivation and learning networks (Schultz 2002). Furthermore, this network is one that has been implicated in ADHD (Rommelfanger and Wichmann 2010). The lack of opportunity for movement leads to decreased chances for forming these important neural connections, potentially causing problems in motivation, attention, and learning in later life.

Down the center of the brain, connecting the two hemispheres, is a thick band of fibers that make up what is called the corpus callosum. This band of fibers is the primary connection between information in the right and left hemispheres of the brain. It is how the two sides of the brain communicate. Information from each side of the body is processed in the contralateral (opposite) hemisphere. So the information from the right side of our body is processed in the left side of the brain. This information, however, must be integrated into a whole, and it does that via the corpus callosum.

One of the developmental goals for young children is the maturation of these connections. This maturation process requires students to move. By bringing movement activities that encourage reaching across the body, or cross-lateral movements, the teacher is actually improving the cortical connectivity between the hemispheres. These types of activities have been attributed to reducing dyslexia (Eden and Moats 2002).

EMBODIED COGNITION

Embodied cognition, the intersection of mind and body, deepens our understanding of learning and has gained attention in educational circles (Gallese and Lakoff 2005; Thelen 1995). Most of our classroom practices teach through lecture and language, utilizing verbal centers of the brain, but a large proportion of the brain is nonverbal. Even in math and science, which primarily map into nonverbal brain regions, we teach new concepts through the terms and scientific jargon. George Lakoff and Rafael Nuñez (2000) discuss in their book, *Where Mathematics Comes From*, how the origins of understanding math must first come out of our embodied mind. So how can teachers use this embodied cognition to better and more fully engage nonverbal neural systems in learning?

Let's take the example of teaching mathematics. Research shows that even young children have a conceptual understanding of proportion, but instead of working with concrete examples, we often bog them down with symbols of fractions. Any teacher will tell you that teaching students fractions can be the most frustrating experience for students and teachers alike. How can we get them to understand?

What embodied cognition does is take advantage of the fact that there are regions of the brain that respond to ratios and proportions. These regions, however, are not in our verbal centers of the brain, so our in vain attempts to explain over and over with words lead us nowhere. However, these regions will respond to visual and concrete examples. Even just having students associate symbols of mathematics with gestures has been shown to improve learning (Cook, Duffy, and Fenn 2013).

Students shown finger symbols indicating chemical structures better understand concepts of how such chemical structures interact (Bivall, Ainsworth, and Tibell 2011). Using gesturing in math improves conceptual understanding and the ability to apply these concepts correctly (Goldin-Meadow, Nusbaum, Kelly, and Wagner 2001). It appears that when we activate these nonverbal brain regions via practices that involve movement, such as gesture, this activation allows concepts to be linked with the verbal representations.

Embodied cognition links auditory, visual, and kinesthetic experiences by fully engaging multimodal systems of the brain. Motor systems have been shown to be linked to perception (Gallese and Lakoff 2005), abstract concepts (Barsalou, Simmons, Barbey, and Wilson 2003), attention/memory (Kosslyn 1995), vision (Blakemore, Bristow, Bird, Firth, and Ward 2005), and language (Olmstead, Viswanathan, Aicher, and Fowler 2009). Embodied cognition can be applied to enhance learning and engage higher-order processes across various content areas.

Although much of the research in embodied cognition has been done in physics, chemistry, and math—disciplines with high abstract conceptual loads—research has also been done showing that simulations of events in history through physical drama, or enactment of stories using props or manipulatives, increase students' memory and ability to draw inferences from stories or historical events (Cooper 2010; Glenberg, Gutierrez, Levin, Japuntich, and Kaschak 2004), and gesturing has been shown to enhance foreign language learning (Macedonia and Knosche 2011).

IMPROVING READING COMPREHENSION

When thinking of embodied practices, reading isn't the first discipline to cross the mind, since typically embodiment is thought of as engaging nonverbal brain regions. However, learning to read is much more than simply decoding. Reading is about comprehension, and comprehension is linked to knowledge of the world around us that is mapped in action and perceptual systems. Hence, students may have an experience or have seen a particular action but are only just beginning to have the language to express it. By engaging the existing knowledge while learning to read new words, the depth of understanding is increased, and learning happens more rapidly and permanently.

This approach may be especially effective for bilingual or English language learners. Students who have some experience or may even have a neural representation of a word in one language can more effectively add new words to that existing neural network by activating the shared visual–motor representation of the common concept. Arthur Glenberg, head of the Embodied Cognition Lab at Arizona State University, developed the program Moved by Reading to maximize students' existing perceptual, emotional, and motor knowledge when learning to read. This program has been able to double reading comprehension in beginning readers (Glenberg 2014). Additional research from his own lab has found that this program is even more effective when working with bilingual children (Restrepo, Adams, Glenberg, Walker, and Danielescu 2014).

To understand why this should be true for bilingual students, think about the fact that our knowledge of the world is mapped in our brains not just through words but also through visual and motor representations. As children develop, a rich background of lived experience becomes available in these perceptual and motor networks. This knowledge is available to draw on in understanding the world; only the bilingual or ELL students do not have the extensive English vocabulary mapped to this experience.

By acting out reading passages, motor and perceptual maps in the brain are activated. This gives ELLs a rich resource of existing knowledge to draw on as they learn new English words. This work is critical given growth in the ELL population in the public schools in the United States, and failure to gain ground in English comprehension may lead to improper identification as learning disabled.

When the students actually moved or acted out the sentence physically in space, for example, pretending to drive a tractor to the farm when reading the sentence "Farmer Bill drove the tractor to the farm," they showed greater learning. But more interestingly still, this same benefit was seen if the students simply imagined they were acting out the sentence. This finding is linked to a body of research in the neurosciences focused on a phenomenon known as mirror neurons. The brain will activate the same motor and perceptual systems through movement or through visualization/imagination of movement.

MOVEMENT, MOTOR SYSTEMS, AND MIRROR NEURONS

Groundbreaking research by Giacomo Rizzolati and colleagues on mirror neurons gave birth to a whole new field of research on the connection between perceptual and motor systems. Mirror neuron refers to the phenomenon that when a person sees an activity, the brain responds as if it has just done the activity. Hence, this research shows that to see an activity stimulates the same neural networks as doing that activity, acting like a mirror to the actual performer (see Rizzolatti and Sinigaglia 2008). Since watching or visualizing an activity activates the same motor areas as engaging in that activity, educationalists have proposed that viewing others' actions or visualized animations should be more effective than static diagrams (de Koning and Tabbers 2011; Decety and Grèzes 2006).

This appears to hold a small kernel of truth, but it depends on how the visualizations are used. In their review of the literature on embodied cognition and visualizations, B. B. de Koning and Huib Tabbers (2011) give several suggestions for increasing the effectiveness of this approach: (1) let the learner follow the movements using gestures, (2) make the learner manipulate the movements through interaction with the animation, (3) embody the movements in the animation using a body metaphor, and (4) stimulate learners to reconstruct the perceptual processing of the movements at the test.

The overarching findings and suggestions all point to the need to intentionally engage the motor systems to obtain the benefits. Movement has been ignored as a critical source of learning until now. Hopefully the growing body of research will help to change the structure of our students' learning experiences to incorporate movement on a regular basis in all classrooms, not just thirty minutes a day of physical education.

MINDFULNESS, RELAXATION, AND STRESS REDUCTION

Movement at school serves a purpose beyond simply increasing learning math or increasing reading comprehension. Movement is critical for preparing the brain to learn. Chapters 12 and 13 cover some of the debilitating cognitive effects of stress in students. Students coming to school from stressful environments have been shown to have higher levels of the stress hormone cortisol. Chronic elevation of cortisol has been shown to damage cells in the hippocampus, a brain region important in learning and memory. Therefore, reducing stress in students is about more than emotional health; it is critical to the biology of learning itself.

Schools are only recently experimenting with practices of mindfulness, meditation, and movement with awareness. To maximize the effectiveness of a program of movement, there is added value in programs that enhance the mind–body connection. Many such programs exist: Feldenkrais, Eutonie, and Holistic Gymnastics are all established practices typically used in physical therapy. Martial arts can aid in developing stillness, self-awareness, and self-control.

Approaches to increasing mindfulness through movement are now entering the schools to great effect. The program Awareness Through the Body (ATB) and the Mind Body Awareness Project have been successfully employed in public schools, and hopefully the positive effects of these new initiatives will pave the way for more such actions. These initiatives are encouraging school leaders to take the time from busy schedules to prepare the students to learn, rather than needing to waste time enforcing punitive actions for misbehavior resulting from stress and poor self-control.

CONCLUSION

Movement is the foundation for building networks of attention, motivation, and executive function (Koch and Ullman 1985). Appropriate learning experiences that include movement engage attention networks. Classroom activities that include movement should become critical components of any curriculum to ensure the full development of attention and working memory systems in the brain. This approach upholds a potential solution to the increasing attention problems, including ADHD, faced by many students in our schools (Rueda, Rothbart, McCandliss, Saccomanno, and Posner 2005).

Embodied practices are excellent approaches to whole classroom activities that can engage learners of all levels. They increase the enjoyment of all learners and target high-risk ELLs to enhance comprehension of new English vocabulary. Movement can and should be integrated into the classroom experience in all subject areas to increase learning and comprehension of abstract concepts. Movement should also be used to prepare the student to learn. Practices of body awareness increase mindfulness and reduce stress. Such practices prime the brain to new learning and reduce misbehavior.

QUESTIONS FOR REFLECTION

1. How can you provide teachers with opportunities to engage students in movement in their classrooms?
2. Has your school taken away movement opportunities in favor of more desk work?
3. Can you bring programs that include embodied cognition of complex phenomenon into your academic disciplines through use of theater space, outside space, or designation of gym areas for large space simulation projects?

10

How Can Memory Be Enhanced?

Linda L. Lyman

"Forgetting is as critical to learning as oxygen."

—Benedict Carey

Some new insights into learning techniques from memory science were elaborated upon in chapter 1, which focused on how learning can be enhanced, but there is more for a principal to consider. What is the relationship between learning and memory? What is the role of forgetting in learning? How can forgetting strengthen learning? How does memory work? Memory is not a single faculty of mind. All thought is physical, embodied—meaning that it happens in the brain in a body. The question this chapter addresses is how can memory be enhanced.

There are different kinds of memory—episodic memories that tell our stories, semantic memories that organize our factual knowledge, and procedural memories that allow us to retain skills. Certain specialized categories of memory exist for things like word retrieval. Different brain systems support different kinds of memory, notably declarative or conscious memory for facts and events, and nondeclarative or unconscious memory for habits and skills.

How is a memory encoded and how is it retrieved? How can learning get from short-term memory to long-term memory? Once in long-term storage how can we access or retrieve what we have learned? Is the challenge for students to learn or to remember, or are they the same thing? Is it the teacher's problem to figure out how to teach for retention? Or is retention the learner's problem? What is working memory?

According to Jerome Rekart (2013), "Teachers facilitate student learning, which only occurs when a memory is created" (xi). He defines a memory as "a skill or information that is persistent, portable (i.e., is carried within the individual), accessible (can be retrieved when needed), and, in the best cases, is usable in a wide array of contexts" (xi). The aim of this chapter is to provide some insights into these opening questions and others.

WORKING MEMORY AND EXECUTIVE FUNCTION

Traditionally, the work of educators has focused on encouraging long-term memories for critical content and facts. However, the goals of twenty-first-century learning focus on building cognitive capacities rather than rote memorization. One such capacity is that of working memory, also referred to as executive function. This may be one of the most highly sought cognitive skills, and programs are just now starting to work on means to build executive functions in our students to assist them in becoming effective learners.

The cellular basis of working memory was first described by Patricia Goldman-Rakic (1995). It was noted that a network in the frontal lobe was always active whenever performing cognitive tasks that required working with information for short periods of time. Unlike long-term memory, which was associated with a permanent inscription in brain areas specific to that particular content, working memory always utilized this particular frontal region regardless of the content. Working memory has since taken on the role of what is termed the central executor, or executive function, which includes inhibitory control and cognitive flexibility.

Currently there is a growing body of research on the factors influencing executive functioning, with some evidence of the ability to improve this much like we can improve intelligence. Furthermore, learning and school success are intimately linked to working memory capacity. The question as to how to build this in our students is one that is only beginning to be understood. Given that executive function in children predicts math and reading competence, as well as self-regulation and social competence, it is not surprising that districts and schools are working to find means of building this ability.

Diamond and Lee (2011) reviewed a list of interventions shown to improve executive function. Although computerized programs show some improvements in working memory, transfer is weak. Diamond and Lee point out that improving executive functioning is really about improving frontal lobe functioning and that frontal lobe function is impaired with stress, loneliness, and poor physical fitness. Approaches that utilize mindfulness practices, martial arts, or even curricular approaches that encourage self-confidence, social bonding, and self-regulation do more to create transferable cognitive skills with long-term gains in executive functioning.

THE FORGET TO LEARN THEORY

An older belief was that a memory not called up or used would disappear from the brain completely over time. This is no longer believed to be true. According to Carey (2014), an emerging theory called the new theory of disuse helps us understand how learning and forgetting are positively interrelated. For example, "forgetting a huge chunk of what we've just learned, especially when it is a brand new topic, is not necessarily evidence of laziness, attention deficits, or a faulty character. On the contrary, it is a sign that the brain is working as it should" (25).

Carey (2014) suggests the name of the new theory should be the forget to learn theory. According to the theory any memory has two strengths, "a storage strength and a retrieval strength" (36). Anything a person has deliberately committed to memory is still stored in memory, but its retrieval strength may be low. Retrieval strength is more limited than storage capacity. We know more than we can retrieve. "Retrieval strength . . . is a measure of how easily a nugget of information comes to mind. Without reinforcement, however, retrieval strength drops off quickly" (37).

Continuing, Carey wrote that the Forget to Learn theory says: "If I stored it, it's in there for good. That is, no memory is ever 'lost' in the sense that it has faded away, that it's gone. Rather, it is not currently accessible. Its *retrieval strength* is low, or near zero" (37). Although it is often frustrating, working hard to retrieve a memory strengthens it for future retrieval.

Carey continues, "The harder we have to work to retrieve a memory, the greater the subsequent spike in retrieval and storage strength (learning)" (38). It is a paradox. He wrote, "Forgetting enables and deepens learning, by filtering out distracting information and by allowing some breakdown that, after reuse, drives retrieval and storage strength higher than they were originally" (40–41). Some breakdown must occur for us to strengthen learning when we revisit the material.

RETRIEVAL CHANGES MEMORIES

Because we can retrieve memories does not mean that we can call to memory every detail exactly as something happened or as we deliberately committed it to memory. The brain has a mind of its own, one might say. Calling forth a memory or retrieving a memory we get "networks of perceptions, facts, and thoughts, slightly different combinations of which bubble up each time. And that just retrieved memory does not overwrite the previous one but then intertwines and overlaps with it" (Carey 2014, 20). In the process of that intertwining, "nothing is completely lost, but the memory trace is altered and for good. As scientists put it, using our memories changes our memories" (20).

That the act of calling up a memory changes the memory is one reason why siblings, for example, can have different memories of how things happened when they were young. Because pieces of a memory are distributed throughout the brain, they do not come together as things happened. Emotions can enter and alter the picture. The brain is a story maker, always seeking patterns that explain the loose facts that come and go. If there are no obvious patterns, the brain will create them—"creating meaning, narrative, cause, and effect" (Carey 2014, 19). Because of these characteristics, each time we call forth a memory a new detail seems to emerge. The brain is not a computer, but more like a language, holding memories together.

MAKING MEMORIES STICK

Several sets of techniques for enhancing memory were presented at a February 2015 conference on memory presented by the Learning and the Brain Society. A presentation by Roddy Roediger, a cognitive scientist who has specialized in memory, was titled "Making It Stick: The Science of Successful Learning and Memory." Through experiments with students of all ages he has developed evidence that self-testing as a form of studying, as well as testing in the classroom, contribute to learning. Testing of memory not only assesses what we know but also changes it. Testing strengthens retention and improves later performance. His work has helped establish the validity of what is called the "spacing effect," which means generally that the greater the spacing between two presentations of information or study sessions, the better is the long-term recall.

Teachers as well as researchers have turned the spacing effect into a practical strategy for learning. Teachers can know, based on research, when the best time is to review key concepts in preparation for an exam, as well as what an optimal schedule for test preparation would be. For middle school, high school, or college, optimal scheduling "basically means you're working with intervals of one day, two days, or one week. That should take care of most situations" (Carey 2014, 78).

In addition to spacing and mixing up practice to make learning stick, Roediger advocates for active learning study strategies, such as participating in study groups, using flashcards, outlining materials, and utilizing memorization techniques. All are better, he says, than rereading material, highlighting material, or reviewing (rereading) notes from class. He has come to believe so strongly in the value of the testing effect to improve memory that he now includes some sort of assessment practice in each meeting of his graduate and undergraduate classes, every day he teaches and every class he teaches.

Roediger's daily class assessments are low stake in terms of students' semester grades but are always graded. The practice permits development of "metacognitive awareness" on the part of the students and in fact lessens test anxiety, he has discovered. The frequent assessments provide retrieval practice that strengthens retention and improves later performance more effectively than does additional study. Another practice Roediger has tested for enhancing learning is giving the final exam on the first and last days of class. Again, his research has established that giving the exam in the beginning contributes to more learning by the end of the course. Cramming works for test preparation, but the learning just does not last beyond the test.

Interestingly, Doyle and Zakrajsek (2013) argue that "the practice of cramming does not meet the neuroscience definition of learning, which requires that learned information be available for use at a later time" (10). Spacing practice, on the other hand, does make learning last. According to Carey (2014), "spaced-out study is as close to a freebie as anything in learning science, and very much worth trying" (79). Interestingly it has been known for over a century that "studying a new concept right after you learn it doesn't deepen the memory much, if at all; studying it an hour later, or a day later, does" (Carey 2014, 68). Distributed, or spaced-learning, practice in certain situations can double the amount you remember later on.

It is a bit of a paradox. Conditions of learning that make performance improve rapidly often fail to support long-term retention and transfer. On the other hand, conditions of learning that appear to create difficulties for the learner, slowing the rate of apparent learning, often increase long-term retention of knowledge. Strategies that help short-term learning often work against long-term retention. Desirable difficulties contribute to learning strength.

Good short-term strategies give the illusion of mastery. They feel good in the short term, like cramming does. We would do well to embrace the concept of desirable difficulties in approaches to increasing learning. Retrieval practice is an example of a desirable difficulty. Is blocked or mixed practice more effective for long-term memory? Textbooks tend to block problems by type, but mixing the problem types is what improves long-term performance. Mixing typically leads to better performance.

STRENGTHENING RETRIEVAL PRACTICES

Ending his presentation at the February 2015 Learning and the Brain Society conference on memory, Roediger summarized five strategies to make learning stick (2015):

1. Practice getting it out versus getting it in
2. Space and mix up practice
3. Try to figure it out before being shown how
4. Elaborate:
   - Connect new learning to what you already know
   - Restate it in your own words
   - Find layers of meaning and cues for retrieval
5. Form mental images and create a narrative

He shared other memory fitness tips, with a list of activities to help enhance memory. These included focus, aerobic exercise, and challenging and meaningful intellectual activity. He emphasized that memory retrieval requires practice.

At the same conference, Milton Dehn, from Schoolhouse Educational Services, LLC, presented a workshop focused on long-term memory strategies. He stressed that interference is the primary cause of forgetting, so memory improves when interference is reduced. Advice includes taking breaks during study so that new information does not interfere with the processing of previous information. Ultimately it is the job of the hippocampus to encode, consolidate, retrieve, and reintegrate memories. "Memories" as cellular components of neural networks can be forgotten through natural cell death (excitotoxicity/apoptosis) or modified through new information. The hippocampus is sensitive to injury, glucose, oxygen, and cortisol levels.

Dehn suggested that teachers try to make it possible for students to visualize verbal information. This sets up two pathways that will then be available for retrieval, but more than two pathways can be set up. Different sensory experiences lead to different pathways. Any can be a key to learning. One way to describe learning, according to the Annenberg Learner website (http://www.learner.org/courses/neuroscience/index.html), is to think of it "as a process that takes information coming into our minds through our senses, so that we can build mental representations of these inputs that remain in our minds even after the sensory inputs have ceased. We call these mental representations 'memories.'"

EFFORTLESS LEARNING

One form of effortless learning happens without thinking when one is sleeping. It seems to be an answer to the questions, what is the sleeping brain doing and why do we sleep at all?

There are at least two theories for why we sleep. One is that sleep functions essentially as a time-management adaptation developed by early humans. Sleeping at night was a way to be alert during the times of day when things were happening and watchful alertness was required.

The other theory is that the primary purpose of sleep is memory consolidation or learning. As Carey (2014) explains the latest research, sleep does not get in the way of learning, but that "unconscious downtime clarifies memory and sharpens skills—that it's a necessary step to lock in both. In a fundamental sense, that is, sleep *is* learning . . . I think of sleep as learning with my eyes closed" (211–212).

What does this mean for the classroom? It means that when we introduce a new concept, we must let the students literally sleep on it. Because the formation of new synapses takes times, letting students work on particular problems over a period of three days will enhance their ability to make connections with prior knowledge. This literal making of new connections will allow for deep discovery and conceptual learning by students. The experiences will last a lifetime and ignite continued engagement and excitement around content areas.

CONCLUSION

Every student deserves a principal who reinforces learning for all who make up the school community. A principal needs to be able to answer the question "What is learning?" Do we define it in terms of what is remembered, or does learning include what we have forgotten?

The answer is both and it makes a difference. "The study of forgetting has, in the past few decades, forced a fundamental reconsideration of how learning works" (Carey 2014, 23). Forgetting is not the enemy of learning. Without some forgetting there would be no benefit of further study. There must be some breakdown of what has been learned so that when we revisit material we can strengthen and deepen the learning.

QUESTIONS FOR REFLECTION

1. How have you experienced memories changing?
2. Do your teachers use frequent low-stakes assessments to develop memory?
3. How do your teachers handle students' forgetting?

III
THE EMOTIONAL CONNECTION

11

Why Is a Positive Learning Environment So Important?

Jennifer McCoy

"We feel, therefore we learn."

—Mary Helen Immordino-Yang and Antonio Damasio

A general Google search of the term "stress" revealed more than 555,000,000 results. Most of the frequently visited sites centered on coping with the physical and emotional effects of stress. In other words, stress is definitely a part of today's culture. Even though positive stress does exist, society is inundated with the negative variety. Negative stress includes overwhelming expectations, commitments, and negative experiences—typically resulting in detrimental effects to people's minds and bodies.

Today's students and staff undergo chronic stress unlike any other generation. Educators must take measures to circumvent the effects of stress in the classroom if they want children to achieve their potential. A positive school environment and quality relationships, among staff as well as between staff and students, can be the difference between student success and failure. Creating a positive environment can be impacted by a variety of factors, including stress, as well as the interplay between emotion and cognition.

STRESS IS DAMAGING TO LEARNING

The damage of chronic stress ultimately impairs a student's ability to perform at high levels. Particularly for children, because parts of the brain responsible for logical thought and planning are still developing, high-stress environments will impair their ability to make good decisions and set goals (Wilson and Conyers 2013). For teens who might have had negative experiences in their early school years, the simple act of attending school can be stressful.

Teachers are faced with "undoing" those negative experiences if they ever hope to build a positive, trusting learning environment. Stress can be an even greater challenge for struggling teens. According to Jensen and Snider (2013), these students' brains are "often overwhelmed by risk factors for academic or social impairment—poverty, parental separation, abuse, neglect, poor nutrition, bullying, lack of housing stability, and health issues" (102).

These same struggling learners are often the recipients of "special programs"—programs implemented under the guise of helping them make academic gains when they are really being force fed a watered-down curriculum. The result is boredom. And boredom comes at a high price. Evidence now shows that boredom can actually contribute to student stress as well as cause behavioral problems due to feelings of hopelessness (Willis 2014).

While all brains, regardless of age, continue to change throughout life, students' brains are not fully developed. Add stress to an undeveloped brain, and this addition quickly slows their progress (Medina 2008). In other words, stressed-out students will struggle with new concepts, and a stressful learning environment will compound that situation. Principals need to keep in mind the potential causes and effects of stress among their students and staff members.

Staff members are just as susceptible to stress as students. According to Hattie and Yates (2014), "Student apathy and lack of motivation are frequently cited as factors underlying teacher stress, burnout, and lack of job satisfaction" (3), thus continuing a vicious cycle for these learning environments. Nevertheless, teachers are expected to build relationships with students, offer nurturing learning environments, convey content in engaging ways, and handle the variety of personalities and needs in their classrooms. Principals can mediate staff stress by circumventing stress factors under their control.

SOME ARE WOUNDED BY SCHOOL

"School wounds . . . are produced in educational environments that are intolerant of cognitive, emotional, or identity differences, where feelings about being different provoke disapproval and shame," wrote Kirsten Olson (2009, 55–56). The wounds being inflicted in schools cannot be easily relegated to just categories of race, class, and gender. She describes how these hidden school lacerations have had devastating and profound spiritual and emotional effects, and she questions whether the traditional industrial assembly line model of education addresses the cognitive and emotional needs of all students.

Olson's interview research lasted over a period of ten years, during which she gathered school stories from across the country. She interviewed "scores of people of all ages, races, ethnicities, and socioeconomic backgrounds; from urban, suburban, and rural communities; people at the top, middle, and bottom of the achievement/success pyramid, in school and in life" (Olson 2009, xii). She began her research with interviews of adults who were quite successful, but soon realized she was hearing an unexpected pattern as persons shared emotionally wounding experiences from schooling that still haunted them:

> Olson certainly expected to hear stories of joyful and productive learning. . . . Instead, she discovered the shadows of pain, disappointment, even cynicism in their vivid recollections of schooling. Instead of the light she expected, she found darkness. And their stories did not merely refer to old wounds now healed and long forgotten; they recalled deeply embedded wounds that still bruised and ached, wounds that still compromised and distorted their sense of themselves as persons and professionals. (xii)

Many described having been treated in demeaning and disrespectful ways. Others described feeling deadened and shamed. Some said the negative messages they received about their abilities made them "toxically rebellious" (28). The long-lasting repercussions of unintentional school wounding provide an argument for moving to a different paradigm. Olson (2009) asks educators to consider how they could create "more cherishing and inclusive school cultures that would incite learning and love" (xiii). Wounding inflicted by the structures, procedures, and environments of schooling can be lessened by redesigned positive environments of caring and empathy.

THE ROLE OF EMOTION IN LEARNING

Good teachers recognize that emotions and feelings affect students' performance and learning. And rightly so, for students' emotional connection to a topic or content area can motivate or demotivate their learning. In essence, students pay attention to instruction that captures their interest at an emotional level. To fully understand how to lead learning, educators need to look into what contributes to cognitive achievement, including the role of emotion.

Two branches of neuroscience are particularly relevant to this topic. Affective neuroscience is the study of the neural mechanisms of emotion, including the psychological study of personality, emotion, and mood. Social neuroscience, on the other hand, focuses on the ways that our brains are hardwired to connect with others. These connections stimulate the neural growth required for learning by fostering emotional attunement.

Two leading neuroscience researchers who bridge both fields are Mary Helen Immordino-Yang and Antonio Damasio, both from the University of Southern California. They agree "that the relationship between learning, emotion and body state runs much deeper than many educators realize and is interwoven with the notion of learning itself" (2007, 3). In an *Education Week* Commentary, Alden Blodget noted that "Damasio . . . has written that 'emotion is the rudder for thought,' and his colleague Mary Helen Immordino-Yang has developed the idea further, stating: 'We think in the service of emotional goals'" (2013). Emotion steers everyone's thoughts, and we think about how new concepts are connected to goals that matter deeply to us.

Additionally, Immordino-Yang (2015) clarifies how our complex emotional states are not separate from our biology, emphasizing also that everyone learns within a cultural frame. Brains do much more than keep people alive physically. Learning literally requires emotion woven into cognition. She wrote:

> Neuroscience has shown us that, in normal health, it is biologically close to impossible for people to think without feeling, or vice versa. Every decoded word, every attempted math problem—just like every lunchtime conversation—is experienced subjectively and evaluated emotionally in terms of a person's own predispositions and memories, even though we are often unaware of these feelings.

Immordino-Yang's research has used neuroimaging techniques to explore the development of empathy. In a series of experiments she has established that when people feel empathy, they are feeling it on the same cells in the brainstem that literally keep them alive. Schwartz (2013) shared Immordino-Yang's research conclusion that "neuroimaging experiments show us that we use the very same neural systems to feel our bodies as to feel our relationships, our moral judgments, and our creative inspiration." We have embodied brains and social minds.

Students, teachers, and administrators must understand how integral emotions are to both thinking and decision making. Consequently, "the aspects of cognition that are recruited most heavily in education, including learning, attention, memory, decision making, motivation, and social functioning, are both profoundly affected by emotion and in fact subsumed within the processes of emotion" (Immordino-Yang and Damasio 2007, 7). A positive environment is important because it fundamentally supports learning at the level of emotion and culture, whereas a negative environment shuts learning down. Schools must engage students positively at the emotional and social levels if they are to make progress at the cognitive level.

WHAT A POSITIVE LEARNING ENVIRONMENT IS . . . AND WHAT IT ISN'T

The good news is that a positive learning environment coupled with affirmative teacher-to-student relationships can improve student learning. Hattie and Yates (2014) explained that "positive teacher-student relationships in the early years (a) predicted reduced levels of externalising and antisocial behaviour in these students, and also (b) served to prevent students . . . from developing long-term trajectories of behavioral problems" (17). However, a school should not expect these changes to happen overnight. The researchers found that the positive results usually took place the year *after* the interventions were implemented.

For anyone envisioning a positive, low-stress learning environment as teachers emulating the sea turtles from *Finding Nemo*, calling students "dude" and telling them to "mellow out," that person would be wrong. Positive learning environments are not about having a *relaxed* attitude in the traditional sense. Students and teachers alike must still be held to high expectations. In fact, students *especially* need high expectations to avoid boredom (Willis 2014). They need consistent activity in the instructional sweet spot of high interest plus challenge, the zone of proximal development, or what some call the level of desirable difficulty.

Students also need to be taught coping skills, and teachers must establish their classrooms as "emotional and social oases" from students' stressful lives. Cervone and Cushman (2014) found that high schools with robust social–emotional learning standards implementation had "strong attendance and low dropout rates, good proficiency results on state assessments, and a high percentage of students going to college" (28).

A positive learning environment is not one in which everyone succeeds all of the time; to the contrary, it is one in which it is *safe* to fail—and learn from it. In this type of classroom, the teacher can use failure as an opportunity to help the student learn—skills, yes, but also how to recover and persevere. When explaining these types of environments, Hattie and Yates (2014) stated that positive student and teacher relationships are "not so much because this is worthwhile in itself, but because it helps build the trust to make mistakes, to ask for help, to build confidence to try again, and for students to know they will not look silly when they don't get it the first time" (21).

A positive learning environment is also balanced. For new information to be learned, teachers need to make *big picture* conceptual sense of something for the students before expecting them to pay attention to and comprehend the details. In other words, sense making comes before detail comprehension. Human brains need breaks to process new concepts. Similarly, teachers must avoid bloated curricula and packed lesson plans. Time for reflective meaning making should be built into the instructional process to aid students in consolidating their learning.

CONCLUSION

A positive learning environment is not merely one more ingredient to student learning; it is *everything* to student learning because emotions are integral to attention and to cognition, to learning and to memory. Through neuroimaging, researchers have been able to see the brain as it learns: "We know now more than ever, that no two brains process information or store data in the same way" (Olson 2009, 124).

The current educational system does not honor neurodiversity by insisting that certain learning goals be achieved at a certain age (e.g., setting a specific age by which all students should read). Lockstep models based simply on age are guaranteed to create a counterproductive mismatch to brain biology. Taking findings of brain research seriously means rethinking how instruction is conceived, including the meaning of disability and implications of neurodiversity. "All brains learn differently" would then take on new meaning.

The goal would be no more unintentional wounding inflicted by the structures, procedures, and environments of schooling. Redesigned positive school environments supporting growth mindsets would be the norm. Educators must redefine their classrooms as havens from the stress in students' lives. Principals must also recognize the role they play in creating and reducing stress for their staff—and in turn, their students. Stress can literally impair brain development and prevent students from learning the material necessary for themselves and their school to be successful. By focusing on positive learning environments, everyone wins.

QUESTIONS FOR REFLECTION

1. How can a principal facilitate a positive learning environment within an educational system filled with so much stress?
2. Does your faculty understand how cognition and emotion are interwoven in the brain and in learning?
3. What are the stories that students in your school would share to describe their experience of school?

12

How Do Trauma and Chronic Stress Affect the Brain?

Stacie M. France

"Traumas produce their disintegrating effects in proportion to their intensity, duration and repetition."

—Pierre Janet

The American Psychological Association defines trauma as an "emotional response to a terrible event like an accident, rape or natural disaster" (Trauma 2014). Traumatic events are typically unexpected, fast-paced events that are over quickly. Immediately after encountering a traumatic event, people may go into shock or denial, while the long-term effects can be "unpredictable emotions, flashbacks, strained relationships and even physical symptoms like headaches or nausea" (Trauma 2014). Although trauma is linked to stress, stress and trauma are not the same.

Short-term stress is a reaction to a brief situation such as meeting a deadline or being stuck in traffic. Long-term stress is different from short-term stress. Examples of long-term stress are living in poverty, coping with dysfunctional families, and being homeless. Although our body reacts to short-term stress, the reaction is short lived. Long-term stress can have more damaging effects, similar to the long-term effects of trauma. For examples, see table 12.1.

OVERVIEW OF BRAIN RESPONSES

It is common knowledge that trauma and chronic stress are hard on human hearts. But how often do we consider how trauma and chronic stress affect the brain, the organ responsible for our thoughts, memories, and learning? When humans become stressed cortisol levels rise, and that decreases our working memory among other things (Kirschbaum, Wolf, May, Wippich, and Hellhammer 1996).

Cortisol is nicknamed the stress hormone because it is excreted by the adrenal glands when we feel even minor stress. High cortisol levels over a prolonged period due to residual stress from trauma or chronic stress can produce several negative effects in the body. Elizabeth Scott,

Table 12.1. Types and Examples of Stress

Trauma	Long-term/chronic stress	Short-term/acute stress

• Emotional and physical response to an unexpected but brief shocking event that causes significant emotional upheaval
• Effects can be long lasting
  • Family violence
  • Witnessing a severe accident
  • Sexual assault
	• Emotional and physical response to being trapped in an unrelenting, miserable, hopeless situation
	• Effects can be long lasting
	  • War
	  • Being stuck in a despised job
	  • Chronic illness
		• Emotional and brief physical response to a short-term circumstance
		• Effects are *not* long lasting
		  • Occasional school-related problem
		  • Being stuck in a long grocery store line

Sources: Sincero (2012), Stress (2014), Trauma (2014)

a stress management expert, identified some of the negative effects of long-term elevated cortisol levels. Her list includes the following: impaired cognitive performance, suppressed thyroid function, blood sugar imbalances such as hyperglycemia, decreased bone density, decrease in muscle tissue, higher blood pressure, lowered immunity and inflammatory responses in the body, and increased abdominal fat (2014).

High cortisol levels produced by trauma and chronic stress are damaging to the body, but what happens to the brain is just as alarming. The hippocampus, which is involved in storing working memory and transferring working memory into long-term memory during sleep, is particularly sensitive to and impaired by high cortisol levels. Therefore, when cortisol levels are high it becomes more challenging to create long-term memories from our working memories. If we cannot remember things effectively due to high cortisol levels, how can we learn? What happens to student achievement when cortisol levels are elevated over a long period of time due to chronic stress and trauma?

Trauma and chronic stress have several distinct effects on the brain. Some of them include decreased nerve cell production in the hippocampus and a reduction in the projections of the neurons, which results in decreases in the overall working ability of the brain. The cortex can even shrink (Klingberg 2013). In terms of brain structure and chemistry, there are three overall effects of childhood trauma. These effects are developmental stagnation, behavior problems, and physiological changes in the brain. Because neurons are designed to change in response to external signals (neuroplasticity), trauma can damage structures and processes in the brain.

Traumatic memories (those that are felt and known) appear to be stored differently and apart from regular memories (those that can be recalled and told as a story). "The unnatural storage of traumatic memory has an impact on one's ability to handle future exposure to adverse situations," according to Jodi Campbell (2015) of the KidsPeace Institute. Students who have suffered trauma can move instantly into the hyperarousal seen in traumatized youth, because they react differently to the amygdala's registering of threat or fear.

"The brain is interpreting every-day stressors as major threats," explained Campbell. As a result we can see troubling behaviors, as traumatized brains can interpret even a small loss or rejection as a new traumatic event and the amygdala shifts into overdrive and experiences a fight or flight urge, for example. When a child is in fact living with trauma, this hyperactive, stressed, and often enlarged amygdala can become the new normal. This can result in a child's making impulsive decisions, verbal or physical aggression, self-harm, and so on.

An enlarged amygdala can lead to greater anxiety in childhood and beyond. Researchers at Stanford have found that the larger the amygdala, the greater amount of anxiety the child experiences, a condition that puts the child at risk for anxiety disorders and depression later in life. Educators need to know these fundamentals about the lasting effects of trauma on the brain and behavior so that our responses are appropriate and we do not unintentionally escalate the trauma reaction.

LAWSUIT ADDRESSING THE EFFECTS OF TRAUMA

As reported in the *Washington Post* blog on May 19, 2015, an unprecedented federal class action lawsuit in California has charged the Compton Unified School District with violating the rights of staff and students by failing to "directly address the trauma that many students experience outside of class that affects their academic performance." Mark Rosenbaum, an attorney for one of the two firms that filed the suit, said in a webcast: "The No. 1 public health problem in the United States today is the effect of childhood trauma on students' opportunity to learn. The widely known, but little addressed scientific fact of life is that childhood trauma can negatively affect the capacity of any child to learn and to succeed in school" (Strauss 2015a).

The suit itself states in part, "Trauma incapacitates by altering the physiology of a child's developing brain, creating a neurobiological response that impairs the performance of daily activities, especially skills essential to receiving an education such as thinking, reading, concentrating, learning, and regulating emotions." The district located in Los Angeles County is being asked to provide better mental health support for students, as well as better training for staff in dealing with student trauma.

The goal of the lawsuit is to shift emphasis in the district away from treating troubled students as "bad children" but rather valuing them as "children to whom bad things happen." Compton is one of the most socioeconomically distressed cities in Southern California, with a high rate of violent crime. The poverty rate is twice the national average, and the murder rate five times the national average. Large numbers of Compton Unified students are likely to benefit from the trauma-sensitive approach sought by this lawsuit.

TRAUMA AND CHRONIC STRESS OF POVERTY

One American study followed 196 children who were raised in homes of poverty. Various indicators of chronic stress and working memory were measured from the age of nine until seventeen. At age seventeen, the working memory of children who were raised in poverty was found to be lower than that of children who were raised in the middle class (Evans and Schamberg 2009). Other researchers, such as Sameroff (1998) and Bowman, Beck, and Luine (2003), have also found that the chronic stress of growing up in a home of poverty reduced academic attainment levels.

In a survey by *Scholastic* conducted in May 2015, the newly named 2015 Teachers of the Year (total of forty-six responded) identified what they would rank as the top three impediments to student learning. They selected family stress (76 percent cited), poverty (63 percent cited), and learning and psychological problems (52 percent cited). One of the award-winning teachers called these impediments to learning "the white elephant in the living room" for educators.

Additionally, clear themes emerged from the study in terms of how teachers see issues and remedies for poverty. They advocated prioritizing funding for things like antipoverty initiatives, early learning, reducing barriers to learning (access to wraparound services, health care, etc.), and professional development/learning in response to rising poverty (Worrell 2015). As of 2015, "for the first time in at least fifty years, a majority of U.S. public school students—51 percent—come from low-income families" (Strauss 2015b).

Many educators recognize the students who come to class hungry or sick or homeless or traumatized or living in wretched conditions as not able to fully concentrate on school tasks. Poverty affects cognition, academic achievement, and mental health. Research on brain development has identified differences in the cognitive and affective neural systems that underlie these effects. Recent brain development and function studies show that poverty affects people from birth to adulthood. However, "conceptual and operational definitions of poverty are unlikely to notice either specific information on the deprivation to which children are subjected, or to associate deprivation with different developmental stages and dimensions" (Lipina and Farah 2011).

Six out-of-school factors common among the poor affect how children learn (Strauss 2015b). These are low birth weight; inadequate medical, dental, and vision care; food insecurity; environmental pollutants; family relations and stress; and neighborhood characteristics. Childhood poverty has the largest effects on the brain's language ability and self-regulatory processing. Psychosocial stress and environmental toxins add to the total stress load carried by children and their families. These factors often work together to increase the damage to the developing child. Typical interventions in the past have been about improving access to medical care or nutritional supplementation.

More recently the focus has come to include programs aimed at training neurocognitive systems directly. According to the CROP Policy brief, "Intervention programs could seek to influence aspects of brain development through strategies that include the training of specific neurocognitive functions and the provision of enriching environments during pre- and postnatal development" (2011).

NEUROCOUNSELING INTERVENTIONS PROMOTE WELLNESS

The field of counseling is moving in the direction of neurocounseling, building a link between counseling and neuroscience (Russell-Chapin and Jones 2014). Counseling has always been a brain-changing practice, so it is not surprising that "mental health counselors are beginning to recognize the power that lies in integrating principles of brain science into daily practice" (20). The need is great. Neuroplasticity allows for negative as well as positive changes in the brain. As Chapin and Russell-Chapin (2014) explain, "Negative neuroplasticity can occur through trauma, repeated negative events, poor environmental conditions, and even constant negative thinking" (5).

The Council for Accreditation of Counseling and Related Educational Programs (CACREP) Standards are moving toward inclusion of neurological and neurobiological foundations. The goal is to be a means for helping clients bridge the gap between brain and behavior. Neurocounseling bridges brain and behavior by illustrating and teaching that physiology has foundational underpinnings of many mental health concerns. Major themes will be strategies for self-regulation, including executive functioning and emotional regulation. School counselors from CACREP-accredited programs will bring this knowledge into their work in schools.

They will have been trained in neurotherapy and neurofeedback as strategies for bringing about greater mental health, including the curing of conditions such as ADHD. For example, Chapin and Russell-Chapin (2014) write that "the value of neurofeedback as a nonmedication treatment for ADHD has been well documented" (174). Studies have been under way for twenty years, and generally neurofeedback has met the criteria for efficacious and specific treatment of ADHD. Informed principals will want to follow the research on the outcomes and efficacy of neurofeedback.

CONCLUSION

Is there hope? Yes, there is absolutely hope for the minds of children who have been exposed to trauma and chronic stress, whatever the cause. But progress will need to be a concerted effort and begin at the level of policy. The human brain is an amazing organ that is constantly changing. The ability of the brain to build new neural circuits and to reorganize itself by forming new neural connections throughout life is the source of hope.

With adequate support in a caring educational community, neuroplasticity allows the neurons (nerve cells) in the brain to compensate for injury and disease and to adjust their activities in response to new situations or to changes in their environment. Although the brains of trauma-exposed or chronically stressed students may be stunted while continually exposed to these difficult circumstances, the brain can recover over time and develop more fully when the amount of stress is reduced. Educators can play a role in that recovery through sensitivity to the social and emotional needs of their students.

QUESTIONS FOR REFLECTION

1. What professional development might be needed to help faculty respond to the stress and trauma being experienced by children, given the rising levels of poverty both in rural and urban areas?
2. How can we create safe places in our schools and classrooms for healing from trauma and chronic stress?
3. How might we expect school counselors to provide support for students suffering from trauma or chronic stress?

13

How Can Stress Be Recognized and Reduced?

Jamie L. Hartrich

"Working hard for something we don't care about is called stress; working hard for something we love is called passion."

—Simon Sinek

For students, stress can take the joy out of learning and replace it with a struggle to excel. Principals need to make sure that schools work at teaching students how to deal with stress in a positive manner. Stress is the body's way of responding to an event we are experiencing that is interfering with our normal equilibrium. Experiencing stress is absolutely normal. Stress isn't all bad; in some instances, it helps the students feel alert, ready, and at their best.

However, in other forms, stress can become toxic to the cognitive learning process, weaken student achievement, decrease self-esteem, depress mood, and prohibit students from flourishing in the classroom. Support of social and emotional health is one of the key factors that students need from a learning environment. Students must have the basic needs of feeling safe, secure, accepted, and free from life stresses to be able to succeed in the classroom.

RECOGNIZING STRESS

Family and school events are the most common causes of stress for children and teenagers. Teachers need to be aware of what is happening in students' lives so they can determine whether they need to help them. Stress can come, for example, from any of the following situations: death of a loved one, divorce of parents, argument with parents, change in living conditions, transfer to a new school, failing grades, absences causing makeup work, active in extracurricular activities, increase in homework, peer relationships, serious argument with close friend, breakup of relationship, or change in sleeping habits (Evans 2014; Jayson 2014; Maldonado 2014; and Wilson and Conyers 2013).

RESPONSES TO STRESS

Warning signs of stress may include the following behaviors depending on the age of the student: accident proneness, anger, anxiety, change in appetite, talking like a baby, attention seeking, hitting, kicking, insomnia, stuttering, biting others, indigestion, thumb sucking, crying spells, detachment issues, excessive aggressiveness, excessive laziness, tattling, respiratory issues, or fingernail biting (Evans 2014; Jayson 2014; Maldonado 2014; and Wilson and Conyers 2013).

When students are under stress, they may experience any number of the types of feelings and thoughts, physical or mental states, in the following list (Evans 2014; Jayson 2014; Maldonado 2014; and Wilson and Conyers 2013):

- Feelings—fear, moodiness, embarrassment, anxiety, irritability
- Thoughts—forgetfulness, fear of failure, self-criticism, difficulty making decisions, peer pressure
- Physical state—sleep deprivation, headache, neck pain, stomach aches, chronic illness, rapid breathing, racing heart
- Mental state—memory loss, inability to concentrate, poor judgment, pessimistic attitude, racing thoughts, constantly worrying

A person's body responds naturally and automatically to stress in typical survival brain mode: fight, flight, or freeze. These ancient responses to threat and fear help cope with danger and discomfort and happen often in classrooms and on playgrounds. An example of a "fight" response might be when a student starts yelling at a friend because of feeling pressured into doing something. "Flight" might be illustrated when a student avoids a situation or leaves unexpectedly because of feeling uncomfortable, perhaps because of perceiving others are thinking or talking about them. "Freeze," a common response, might be displayed when a teacher calls on someone in class to answer a question and the student's mind goes blank and he or she can hardly breathe or move. Additional examples of behavioral symptoms of stress reflecting the natural fight, flight, or freeze responses may include the following (Wolfe 2001):

- Fight—crying, punching, tight jaw, grinding teeth, glaring, fight in the voice, yelling, kicking, feet stomping
- Flight—restless legs, anxiousness, shallow breathing, darting eyes, running away from the situation, fidgety, looking trapped, tense
- Freeze—immobile, staying stuck in one place, pale skin, appearing numb, stiff or slow-moving legs, holding breath, heart pounding, fear in the eyes

REDUCING STRESS

Proactive principals understand the importance of teaching social and emotional skills. Social and emotional learning (SEL) supports and provides a platform for academic success. According to the Collaborative for Academic, Social, and Emotional Learning (CASEL), effective programs exist at all levels, from classroom focused to school wide. Because of changing times, social and emotional resources are important to the future health and well-being of students of all ages.

According to Lopes and Salovey (2004) effective SEL programs should be theoretically based, comprehensive, and integrated into the curriculum as well as extracurricular activities: "They should promote a caring, supportive, and challenging classroom and school climate, teach a broad range of skills; be undertaken by well-trained staff with adequate, ongoing support; promote school, family, and community partnerships; and be systemically monitored and evaluated" (77). Teachers can work with enriching classroom instruction with social and emotional learning whether or not a school-wide program exists. School-wide programs are a more comprehensive way, however, to promote positive youth development.

Prior to Goleman's (1995) work on emotional intelligence, Salovey and Mayer (1990) developed a theory of emotional intelligence revolving around four basic abilities: (1) perceiving emotions, (2) understanding emotions, (3) using emotions in thought, and (4) managing emotions in behaviors. Now that more is known about the brain and the centrality of emotion to learning, educators must give attention to the emotional connections among students, staff, and family members.

Lopes and Salovey (2004) conclude that "managing our emotions, and relating to others, are among the greatest challenges that we face in life. Helping children to face these challenges may not be easy, but it is essential that we try" (89). Chapin and Russell-Chapin (2014) practice neurotherapy and neurofeedback as clinicians to enhance self-regulation of clients. They write, "When properly functioning, our brain is self-regulating. It helps us navigate the demands of life, allowing us to cycle as needed between states of calmness and alert" (54). Unmanaged stress can lead to impaired self-regulation.

There are many ways to manage stress. As adults, we understand when we are becoming stressed and know how to relieve our stress levels. Students may or may not have any understanding of stress or ways to deal with it. Because each person is so different and many ways exist to relieve stress, figuring out what works best for each individual is imperative (Wilson and Conyers 2013).

Identifying and acknowledging the causes of stress and expressing feelings are the most effective tools for students to reduce stress. Table 13.1 is a compilation of approaches to stress reduction from several sources. Students who practice these skills when stressed can learn how to cope, regulate their behaviors, and feel better. Each teacher and student in a school would benefit from learning and practicing stress management skills and exercises such as those described in table 13.1.

Table 13.1. Stress Management Skills and Exercises

Stress Management Skills and Exercises	Source
Deep-Breathing Exercise • Hands at your side. • Relax your body. • Close your eyes. • Breathe in slowly and deeply through your nose, making your diaphragm grow. • Exhale slowly through your mouth. • Put your hand on your lower abdomen to make sure you are breathing correctly. • Repeat 10 times.	Russell-Chapin and Jones (2014)
Deep Muscle Relaxation • Students will be asked to tighten and relax different muscle groups. • Students may sit or lie on their backs. • Start with the head and move down to the feet. • Example: Muscles in forehead—wrinkle forehead, try to touch your eyebrow to your hairline . . . hold for 5 seconds . . . and relax.	Jayson (2014)

Simple Meditation
• Sit comfortably, balanced and relaxed.
• Breathe slowly, deep abdomen breathing.
• Practice a few deep breaths.
• All of the following actions are done silently:
  • Rotate head in easy, slow circles; change directions.
  • Look up; tilt head back. Look down; put your chin on your chest.
  • Drop your arms and hands to your side and shake gently.
  • Raise your feet off the floor and gently shake your knees.
  • Straighten your spine.
• Teacher will say, "Close your eyes."
• Relax your mind and do not think.
• Teacher will say, "Open your eyes."
• Repeat the eye closing and opening a few more times.
	Jayson (2014)

Visual Imagery • Students sit with their eyes closed. • Using a calm, quiet, slow voice, give your class a visual scenario to imagine. • Example: Imagine you are on a beach—you feel the wind blowing in your hair, the sand is warm on your feet, the water is cool and wet, and you hear birds chirping in the background and the waves hitting the rocks . . . • Before you finish, using a visual scenario, have the students leave their problems at their visual place. • Example: You are at the edge of the ocean, you feel the heavy pull on your back. You pull and throw whatever is bothering you off your back. The weight is gone and you are watching that heavy rock sink into the ocean . . . • Allow students to share verbally or in a journal activity the experience they felt throughout the activity.	Ostroff (2012)
Peer Sharing • Students have the opportunity to share thoughts and feelings within a safe and structured activity. • Place students into pairs. Student 1 talks while student 2 listens.	Wilson and Conyers (2013)

- After about 1–3 minutes, students switch roles.
- After sharing is complete, regroup students into groups of three.
- Student 1 talks while students 2 and 3 listen.
- After 1–3 minutes students switch roles.

Movement to Music Freeze Dance — Wilson and Conyers (2013)
- Students find a safe place to move/dance in classroom.
- Students move to the music.
- Students freeze when the music stops.
- When music starts again, students move to match the music.
- Activity involves only movement, no talking.
- Idea is to move from fast-moving music to slow, calming music.

CONCLUSION

Living with stress is a reality in the twenty-first century. If we are not proactive, stress will damage our brains by default, reducing our resilience and robbing us of joy. In a professional development meeting for educational leaders at the Harvard Graduate School of Education, 89 percent of those attending said they felt overwhelmed; 84 percent confessed that they neglected to take care of themselves in the midst of stress; and 80 percent reported scolding themselves when they performed less than perfectly (Brown and Olson 2015, 4).

Stress reduction must begin with principals. We cannot lead from the fullness of our hearts and minds unless we are also taking care of our bodies and making time to enjoy being alive. Even though the position of principal is almost by definition stressful, still much stress is self-imposed. As principals, we need to be alert to unchecked stress in the lives of our teachers and students and take needed action to change priorities. How we feel is shaping how we think. When we reduce stress for ourselves the entire school feels the difference.

QUESTIONS FOR REFLECTION

1. How do we recognize when faculty and staff are stressed?
2. How are teachers striving to create stress-free environments in classrooms?
3. How does the school's overall climate and culture contribute to or reduce stress?

14

How Do the Arts Nurture and Connect Emotions?

Patricia M. Valente

"Every child is an artist; the problem is staying an artist when you grow up."

—Pablo Picasso

Human imagination starts from widespread connections in the brain that collectively manipulate ideas, images, and symbols. Creativity in art, science, music, and other fields requires the ability to put together different mental representations to form new ones. More complex cognitive processes, like imagination or creative thinking, do not work in separation between brain areas; rather there is communication of the entire brain. Because thinking is an emotional process, the arts are uniquely positioned to make an important contribution to emotional awareness and health. Students' emotions are biologically intertwined with their thinking.

CREATIVITY AND THE BRAIN

Imagination and creativity require and integrate a broad network of brain areas. In particular, a network of four core brain areas—the occipital cortex, the posterior parietal cortex (PPC), the posterior precuneus, and the dorsolateral prefrontal cortex (DLPFC)—are involved in visual processing, attention, and executive functions (Lewis 2013). Neuroscientists continue to find evidence as to how the mental and physical activities required for the arts are central to brain function. Certain brain regions are sensitive to or specialized for music, while others are devoted to initiating and coordinating movement in dance. Drama stimulates specialized networks that focus on spoken language and emotions. Visual arts excite the internal visual processing system to recall reality or create fantasy with the same ease (Sousa 2006).

ARTS INTEGRATION

Research studies have found that the most powerful effects on brain function occur in programs that integrate the arts with subjects in the core curriculum. Researchers suggest that arts integration causes both students and teachers to rethink how they view the arts and generates conditions, including the following, that are ideal for learning:

- Students have a greater emotional investment in their classes.
- Students work more diligently and learn from each other.
- Cooperative learning groups turn classrooms into learning communities.
- Parents become more involved.
- Teachers collaborate more.
- Art and music teachers become the center of multiclass projects.
- Learning in all subjects becomes attainable through the arts.
- Curriculum becomes more authentic, hands on, and project based.
- Assessment is more thoughtful and varied.
- Teachers' expectations for their students rise.

HIGHER ACADEMIC PERFORMANCE

Dana Arts and Cognition Consortium brought together neuroscientists to wrestle with the question of why training in the arts has been associated with higher academic performance and to understand the relationship between arts training and the ability of the brain to learn in other cognitive domains. Figure 14.1 summarizes what they learned. Reports can be downloaded at www.dana.org.

The Dana Arts and Cognition Consortium developed a theory about how arts training might work to enhance cognition. The theory resulted in identification of five facets: (1) there are spe-

An interest in a performing art leads to a high state of motivation that produces the sustained attention necessary to improve performance, as well as the training of attention that leads to improvement in other domains.
Specific links exist between high levels of music training and the ability to manipulate information in both working and long term memory; these links extend beyond the domain of music training.
In children, there appear to be specific links between the practice of music and skills in geometrical representation.
Correlation exists between music training and both reading acquisition and sequence learning.
Training in acting appears to lead to memory improvement through the learning of general skills for manipulating semantic information.
Learning to dance by effective observation is closely related to learning by physical practice, both in the level of achievement and also the neutral substrates that support the organization of complex action. Effective observational learning may transfer to other cognitive skills.

Figure 14.1. Relationship of Arts Training and Cognitive Ability

cific brain networks for different art forms; (2) there is a general factor of interest or openness to the arts; (3) children with high interest in the arts, and with training in those arts, develop high motivation; (4) motivation sustains attention; and (5) high sustained motivation, while engaging in conflict-related tasks, improves cognition (Posner, Rothbart, Sheese, and Kieras 2008).

Neuroscientists from the Dana Arts and Cognition Consortium believe that any training that truly engages the interest of the child and motivates the child can serve to help train attention. Their findings indicate that arts training could work through the training of attention to improve cognition for those with an interest and ability in the arts. The attentional brain network is related to self-regulation of cognition and emotion. Executive attention plays an important role in the child's everyday control of thoughts, feelings, and behavior.

VISUAL ARTS AND THE BRAIN

The human brain is wired in such a way that it can make sense of lines, colors, and patterns on a flat canvas. Artists throughout human history have figured out ways to create illusions, such as depth and brightness, that aren't actually there but make works of art seem somehow more real (Landau 2012).

It goes without saying that most paintings and drawings are two-dimensional. Yet the brain knows immediately if there's a clear representation of familiar aspects of everyday life, such as people, animals, plants, food, or places. Several elements of art trick the brain into interpreting meaning from the arbitrary. Artistic training assists students to develop problem-solving skills.

Elliot Eisner (2002), a lead researcher on the value of art education to public schooling, argues that it is essential for educators to allow ample space in the day for students to use their imagination to develop meaning of concepts and explore the world around them. He continues to explain that the ability of students to form concepts and to represent these concepts reflects the use and growth of the mind: "The arts invite children to pay attention to the environment's expressive features and to the products of their imagination and to craft a material so that it expresses or evokes an emotional or feelingful response to it" (23).

MUSIC AND THE BRAIN

What has been found for musicians is not that their memory is better; rather it is that they apply strategies of rehearsal to maintain information in memory more effectively. Rehearsal is a way to implement an attentional strategy, in the sense defined by "executive attention" or executive function. Rehearsal plays into the strengthening of the brain's executive functions, including the ability to strategize, retain information, regulate behavior, solve problems, and adjust plans to changing mental demands. Research on the connections between music training and executive function found increased activity in the supplementary motor area and prefrontal cortex of musicians' brains.

Effects of Musical Training on Verbal Memory

Musicians scored better compared to the nonmusicians on a test of long-term verbal memory, but this advantage disappeared when the musicians were prevented from rehearsing the material. Evidence found that the musicians had a greater span of verbal working memory compared to the nonmusicians. The greater verbal working memory span was enhanced by the use of rehearsal skills in musicians, rather than a result that could be attributed to a hardwired difference in verbal memory capacity. This result suggests that musical training has the added benefit of training another cognitive skill, rehearsal, which has spillover effects onto cognitive tasks that engage verbal memory.

The musicians appear to be more able to rehearse the verbal memory, and this is what causes greater engagement of the brain's medial temporal lobe structures, as a mechanism to bind the items to the context in which they occur. In fact, children with one to five years of musical training were able to remember 20 percent more vocabulary words read to them off a list than children without such training.

That's especially compelling because highly developed verbal memory skills have numerous applications in nonmusical contexts, such as helping students learn and remember content from speeches and lectures. Musicians who began their training as children have also been shown to learn new languages more quickly.

Cognitive Systems That Underlie Music and Mathematical Abilities

Three core systems at the foundation of mathematical reasoning are: (1) a system for representing small exact numbers of objects (up to three); (2) a system for representing large, approximate numerical magnitudes; and (3) a system for representing geometric properties and relationships. Each system emerges in infancy, continues into adulthood, and is malleable by specific experiences.

Students' mastery of formal mathematics depends on these three systems and their relationships. Music training fosters mathematical ability by activating and enhancing one or more of these systems. In addition, music training could activate and enhance processes that connect these systems. Intensive music training is associated with improved performance in the core mathematical system for representing abstract geometry.

DANCE AND THE BRAIN

Research from the Dana Arts and Cognition Consortium indicates that dance training can enable students to become highly successful observers. They found that learning to dance by watching alone can be highly successful and that the success is sustained at the neural level by a strong overlap between brain areas that are used for observing actions and also for making actual movements. These shared neural substrates (a part of the nervous or brain system that underlies a specific behavior or psychological state) are critical for organizing complex actions into sequential structure (Gazzaniga et al. 2008):

> Toes tap, wrists flick, arms extend, but it is the brain that dances. Many parts of the brain act together to turn a body's motion from discrete movements into a fluid, physical art form. Watching or executing a moment of dance, several regions of the brain may become active: they may speedily calculate spatial orientation, readjust motor signals, or attach emotional responses to the choreography. (Bates 2014)

Planned movements start in the motor cortex. This region is divided into sections that control different parts of the body. Signals from the motor cortex travel to the spinal cord, then to an arm or finger, telling it to move a certain way. The more precise the movement, the greater the area in the motor cortex devoted to the movement. "The brain must coordinate all its effort for the joints and muscles to contract to the perfect degree, to achieve a rhythmic, well-coordinated style of dance" (Bates 2014).

DRAMA AND THE BRAIN

Mirror neurons have been found to play a key role in developing self-awareness and social connection. Drama has been known as a mirror to the human condition because of asking questions and reflecting on aspects of how we understand and relate to ourselves and each other. Drama appears to use mirror neurons. Through the reenactment of dramatic circumstances, children are able to delve deeper into a "level of self-perception and social understanding regarding those circumstances" (Batema 2014). Drama includes role-playing, directing, scripting, improvisation, costume, set design, and other forms of creative expression. Drama gives children a chance for self-expression, positive attention from peer groups, and cognitive and emotional development.

Awareness of Emotions

The actor's development of attention and concentration cultivates the capacity to be aware of feelings. There are three main aspects of emotion: the first is the amygdala's influence on the cortex (conscious/cognitive processing); the second is arousal triggered by the amygdala (attention/implicit memory); and the third is bodily feedback (visceral and autonomic responses/states). Without these three components, a person cannot experience emotion (fear). The basic concentration and attention exercises that actors begin their training with help build observation and develop human consciousness, which aids in developing capacity to being aware of one's feelings (Brassard 2008).

Verbal Memory

Verbal memory is increased because actors are able to apply strategies for pulling out semantic themes from verbal material and these strategies result in better memory for the material in question. It is a matter of strategy and a matter of applying attention to semantic themes rather than the word-for-word memorization that we sometimes associate with verbal memory.

The universality of themes in drama draws in actors and audience alike at the fundamental level of human emotion. The semantic themes are intentionally entwined in the episodes of the play, leading to deeper meaning and memory. Watching the enactment of emotion on the stage captures our attention and makes possible the vicarious experience of emotion.

CONCLUSION

The arts play an important role in human development, enhancing the growth of cognitive, emotional, and psychomotor pathways. Schools have an obligation to expose children to the arts at the earliest possible time and to consider the arts as fundamental (not optional) curriculum areas. Finally, learning in the arts provides a higher quality of human experience throughout a person's lifetime. Emotions matter to meaningful learning, and the arts have the ability to open students to deeper understanding of themselves and others.

QUESTIONS FOR REFLECTION

1. How might the arts play a stronger school role in developing and nurturing social and emotional learning?
2. What are teachers doing to integrate the arts into their teaching practices?
3. How can principals encourage the use of the arts in classrooms to support Common Core standards?

IV

THE BRAIN ON SCHOOL

15

How Can Mindset Make Someone Smarter?

Matthew K. Heid

"You can be as smart as you want to be."

—Carol S. Dweck

A child is born to learn. It seems to happen naturally in the beginning. Ultimately, though, much of what can be or is learned by a person is determined by mindset, defined by Doyle and Zakrajsek (2013) as "your view about your own intelligence and abilities" (86). A mindset develops through experiences over time.

Carol Dweck (2006) is the psychologist and researcher whose work popularized the concept of mindset to explain why some persons succeed and others do not. Her decades of research established mindset regarding intelligence as falling into one of two categories: a *fixed* or a *growth* mindset. These mindsets can manifest at any age. Teachers as well as students can display characteristics of either mindset. Mindsets can be changed.

A FIXED MINDSET

Individuals with a fixed mindset believe that their intelligence is simply an inborn trait— they have a certain amount, and that's that. Persons who have fixed mindsets typically are discouraged about their potential. As suggested by Dweck (2010), some characteristics of persons who have a fixed mindset include:

- They believe that failure is disastrous and looks poorly on them, and thus they will avoid doing anything that takes a chance at failure.
- They choose not to put in a great amount of effort at tasks for fear that effort will lead to failure and be wasted time.
- They tend to blame their failures on other people and see the success of others as making them look bad.
- They take criticisms as personal attacks.
- They tend to value looking smart above all else.

A GROWTH MINDSET

Contrasting with a fixed mindset is a growth mindset. Individuals with a growth mindset believe that they can develop their intelligence over time. People who develop a growth mindset tend to model these characteristics:

- They value criticism as a way to get better.
- They are happy about the success of others.
- They value hard work and effort.
- They look at failures as new opportunities to learn.
- They believe with hard effort they can achieve.

These two different mindsets can affect the quality of teaching and learning that takes place in any school. In school, students with a growth mindset are much more likely to succeed at more difficult content because they are willing to take the risk of failing. They are willing to learn from those failures until they succeed, whereas a fixed-mindset student for example would likely not take the difficult AP Chemistry class. Another scenario is that the student would take it and then drop it because of fear of failure.

MINDSET AND GROWTH IN THE CLASSROOM

So how can these concepts apply to teaching and learning in a classroom? Teachers who understand the neuroplasticity of the brain are more likely to operate from a growth mindset themselves and foster that in their students. If a teacher dismisses neuroplasticity of the brain as speculation or does not believe that brains are malleable and growing and changing throughout life, then that fixed mindset will be obvious in classroom practices, interactions with the students, and willingness to undertake change in the classroom. A growth mindset on the part of a teacher contributes positively to students reaching their potential. A teacher's growth mindset can make a student smarter because brains respond to positive beliefs, care, and acceptance.

Students respond with growth from a greater sense of well-being when a teacher transmits positive beliefs about what each of them can learn and do. Teachers who believe that intelligence is fixed at birth tend to communicate that some are smart and others are not. This attitude contributes to students' discouragement and lack of effort rather than to their potential for growth. On the other hand, a teacher who has a growth mindset and teaches metacognitive strategies (see chapter 3) can turn a classroom of students around. A growth mindset can take root when students become aware that they can learn how to learn. It is a mindset that responds to nurturance and caring relationships. Teaching metacognitive strategies can enable a student to move from a fixed to a growth mindset and can completely transform a mind and ultimately a life.

Dweck (2010) argues that teachers need to create a growth mindset culture for success in the classroom. She suggests the best ways to do this are:

- To educate students about fixed and growth mindsets
- To encourage students by emphasizing that learning takes time
- To give encouragement and praise for the success that students do have

- To set challenging goals
- To "emphasize challenge not success"
- To use the words "not yet" instead of the word "fail" to describe outcomes

Educational leaders need to ensure that educators' professional development includes gaining knowledge of fixed versus growth mindsets and understanding the importance of growth mindsets in the classroom for themselves and their students. Principals need to encourage students and teachers, but also to challenge them. Students need to know that it is okay to take risks and fail because that is all part of the learning process. "We learn by our mistakes!" is a belief that is part of having a growth mindset.

MINDSET, BOREDOM, AND MISBEHAVIOR

Students with fixed mindsets are vulnerable to disengaging from the classroom learning processes and manifesting boredom or chronic misbehavior. Judy Willis (2014) stated that "the most frequent reason now given by high school students who drop out is boredom" (28). She suggests that boredom is caused by a set of factors. These range from not being intellectually satisfied to being too stressed out by a broad range of materials. Both of these situations can lead to boredom. A fixed mindset can cause a person to go through the motions of school disengaged. Students who are disengaged are easily subject to boredom. Boredom is a major concern for teachers and educators. A student who is bored is likely a student who is not learning and who, from boredom, can act out with unacceptable behaviors that are problematic for everyone.

From her background as a neurologist, Willis (2014) offers a way to help students understand why they are bored and choose to respond reflectively rather than reactively. She wrote:

> The ability to evaluate one's emotions before responding to a trigger is a uniquely human trait. However, this reflective response can only take place if the overall emotional state of the individual is not in a high-stress mode. Teachers can help students lower the resistance that builds in their minds when they attribute their frequent academic or behavioral failures to their own fixed abilities. When students learn about their brains' emotional filter, they understand that bad behavior doesn't mean they're bad people without the potential to grow. (31)

There are some other solutions that may help solve the problem of boredom. Boosting relevance and novelty in the classroom can get the attention of students who have disengaged. Increasing the challenge of the material so that it has a desirable difficulty will usually decrease boredom as well as increase the feeling of achievement. If students are taught that they can control their own mindsets and that mindset is a choice, they will be more able to overcome emotions such as boredom. Students can learn more through recognizing and overcoming a fixed mindset. Teaching metacognition is a good strategy for mitigating many of the challenges that can be seen in classrooms every day and helping students take ownership of their own learning.

METACOGNITION + GROWTH MINDSET = SMARTER

New social psychology research at Stanford University and elsewhere involving larger and more rigorous field trials is providing evidence that students benefit from learning that intelligence is not fixed (Chen 2014). For example, one study involved 1,594 students at thirteen US high schools, including 519 participants who were all underperforming teens with the lowest GPAs. The underperforming students were equally divided between the two treatment groups. Each group was told only that the presentation they experienced was part of a general study of how and why students learn.

The total number of students (1,594) were divided into two treatment groups. Half of the high school students participated in watching a thirty-minute online lesson explaining the basic anatomy of the brain. They had no other experiences. During the same thirty-minute time period the other half of the students had a different experience. In this group, each person first read an article that described scientific evidence of the brain's malleability. Then the group watched an online presentation explaining that people can get smarter by working out their brains, just like people get stronger by working out their muscles.

Different study strategies for getting smarter were explained in the conclusion of their thirty-minute experience. Then they were asked to summarize what they'd learned by composing a note of advice to a hypothetical struggling student. Here is what one student who participated in this second experiment group wrote in a note of advice to that hypothetical student:

> The more you practice or study the more you learn. Your brain has neurons inside that grow whenever you learn something new. Even though you may struggle in a certain subject the neurons in your brain are making new connections and your brain is getting stronger and smarter. . . . Struggling in school is absolutely normal and we may feel and call ourselves "dumb" during these times. If you practice using better ways to study and learn you will get smarter and might struggle less. (Chen 2014)

This intervention happened early in the spring semester 2012. By the end of the spring term, the proportion of those who earned satisfactory grades rose to 49 percent from the 43 percent the previous semester. This represented a relative gain of 14 percent. Researchers were satisfied with these numbers because students who don't perform well early in the year usually continue to do worse and are at risk of dropping out of school. The hope is that the participants in the mindset intervention will be more likely to actually graduate from high school. One of the researchers cautioned that "academic mindset interventions are not magic bullets."

In a more recent *Education Week* article also published online, Dweck (2015) wrote about some common pitfalls and misunderstandings that have developed as her mindset work has been applied. She emphasized that a growth mindset isn't just about effort, calling that the most common misconception. The goal is to have learning result from the effort. For learning, students need to try new strategies and not be satisfied with having put forth a lot of effort. The effort is a means to an end.

In another implementation misconception, Dweck has seen the fixed mindset label given to a child and used to blame or justify why a child is not learning. "The growth mindset was intended to help close achievement gaps, not hide them," she wrote. She has observed that many teachers and parents have claimed a growth mindset but not followed through on it in classroom or parenting practices. This *false* growth mindset could describe teachers who simply praise the effort and parents who consider the mistakes children make as signs of failure rather than opportunities to learn.

Dweck's (2015) article suggests recognizing that we are all a combination of fixed and growth mindsets. She advises, "If we want to move closer to a growth mindset in our thoughts and practices, we need to stay in touch with our fixed-mindset thoughts and deeds." Referring to her colleagues in the mindset work, she concluded, "Maybe we made the development of a growth mindset sound too easy. Maybe we talked too much about people having one mindset or the other, rather than portraying people as mixtures. We are on a growth-mindset journey too."

CONCLUSION

In concluding this chapter, we offer suggested strategies principals can encourage to create a growth mindset culture. The strategies are excerpts from Carol Dweck's guest response on Larry Ferlazzo's (2012) *Education Week* blog:

1. Establish high expectations (not just high standards). [L]et students know that you are challenging them *because* you know all of them have the ability to meet those expectations.
2. Create a risk-tolerant learning zone. Let your students know that you value challenge-seeking, learning, and effort above perfect performance, and that . . . mistakes are to be expected and that we can all learn from them.
3. Give feedback that focuses on process—the things students can control, like their effort, challenge-seeking, persistence, and good strategies . . . and the importance of their own actions in achieving success.
4. Introduce students to the concept of the malleable mind . . . that neuroscience shows that our brains develop through effort and learning.

Researchers have established that students with a growth mindset have greater motivation and higher achievement levels than students who believe their abilities are fixed. That higher achievement, or getting smarter, results from students sustaining effort and trying multiple strategies until something works. Teachers can influence a student's mindset through what they say and do in the classroom. Teachers are encouraged not to settle for effort itself, but to be prepared to introduce students to different strategies in response to learning challenges.

QUESTIONS FOR REFLECTION

1. How can principals recognize when teachers have fixed mindsets about their own abilities?
2. In what ways can a principal encourage teachers to adopt a growth mindset with all their students?
3. How can principals respond when teachers' practices display the belief that intelligence is fixed and they seem to treat students accordingly?

16

How Can Knowing about Brain Science Improve Reading?

Patricia M. Valente

"Reading to the mind is what exercise is to the body."

—Joseph Addison

Reading is not a natural part of human development like oral or spoken language development is. Unlike learning to speak through observations and imitation, reading takes multiple regions of the brain simultaneously working together through networks of neurons. Major concepts explored in this chapter are patterning strategies, fluency building, vocabulary building, and comprehension, followed by attention to dyslexia.

Think of the tasks needed to go from connecting symbols to sounds, sounds to words, words to meaning, meaning to memory, and memory to thoughtful information processing. Understanding the brain activity during the different stages of learning to read will help schools use specific strategies that will improve instruction in teaching the many components of reading.

Neuroimaging has created opportunities to study how we learn to read. Learning to read is complex and demanding. Researchers are finding it is a richly coordinated process that connects a variety of brain regions. Many studies have confirmed that reading difficulties are often caused by specific brain-based differences in how children process information.

By using brain imaging to study reading, psychologists and their colleagues in medicine and education can collaborate to develop research-based teaching approaches that significantly improve how students learn to read. There is now evidence that effective instruction in reading normalizes brain function. With targeted interventions, brains can change in as little as a year, which means that most kids who are at risk for reading problems can still learn to read.

THREE PROPOSED BRAIN SYSTEMS AND PATHWAYS CONNECTED TO READING

Neuroimaging studies have found three neural systems to be most active during reading: the frontal reading system, ventral posterior processing system, and the dorsal posterior reading system. These systems are elaborated in figure 16.1.

> **The frontal reading system** is connected to word analysis or phonological and semantic processing. The Broca's area is also found in this system. The Broca's area is involved in language processing, speech production, and comprehension.
>
> **The ventral posterior processing system,** found in the occipital and temporal lobes, is connected to visual-phonological connection or the visual and pattern for words.
>
> **The dorsal posterior processing system** includes parts of the parental and temporal lobes. This system is connected to word analysis by the visual features of the word. It has been noticed in early reading and recognized in the brain in the analysis of words by linking letters to sounds.

Figure 16.1. Brain Systems and Pathways Connected with Reading

Neuroimaging demonstrated the interdependency of these different brain regions and the importance of each of the multiple regions working successfully together for students to develop reading skills.

PHONOLOGICAL PROCESSING

An important part of learning to read is being aware of the smaller sounds that represent letters and words. Phonological awareness is the process of recognizing individual sounds that make up words as well as identifying the word that is made up of those individual sounds. This process takes place naturally and instinctively in spoken language, whereas in reading, the process requires the understanding that the written word is made of letters that are intentionally related to segments of spoken words.

Unlike spoken language, reading must be learned at a conscious level. Judy Willis (2008) states, "Students need to learn the phonological processing of reading and recognize that specific sequence of letters represent the phonological structure of words" (19). This forms the base for learning to read and identify patterns. Scanning with fMRI has indicated that certain brain regions are more active than others in phonological processing. Dyslexia is considered to be a phonological processing problem or variation in the brain.

MANIPULATING PATTERNS TO IMPROVE READING

The brain naturally seeks to find patterns and evaluate the significance of the incoming data. "Effective reading instruction that corresponds to the brain's patterning process results in more successful and effective learning," writes Willis (2008, 22). The brain sorts out the data that it is receiving and then focuses attention on the information that it determines to be most valuable at that moment. If the patterns in letters, words, or sentences are not clear to students, then they are less likely to connect new information with existing information.

Patterning helps to organize the incoming information. If students are unable to recognize the pattern, they may not successfully direct information to the executive functioning frontal lobe brain region. There working memory pairs the new information with the existing information and codes the items into long-term memories, a process that develops reading skills. Pattern instruction and recognition are essential parts of learning to read.

IMPROVE READING FLUENCY

Another essential part of learning to read is fluency. Fluency is the ability to read a text with expression, accurately and at the speed of speech. While reading, students are able to decode accurately and rapidly, automatically group words, and scan ahead for punctuation cues. Students pause and change voice or pitch while reading fluently, imitating natural conversation. According to Willis (2008), "Fluency appears to be related to neural patterning from the visual sensory intake and printed word processing areas in the occipital lobes" (47).

Practicing reading will build up the neural circuits that rapidly decode the written word, enabling students to decode, recognize punctuation, and comprehend the meaning of the text all at the same time. As students practice their reading they will increase their neural processing efficiency and read with better expression and comprehension. Willis (2008) uses group learning strategies, which include rapid naming practice, repeated reading, guided rereading, modeling, and choral reading.

VOCABULARY

Possessing a rich vocabulary at a young age is a good predictor of success in learning to read. Willis (2008) writes, "Rich vocabulary reflects success in almost every region of the brain, from rote memory through working and relational memory, categorizing, connecting, patterning, storage, and executive function" (80). These processes of executive function are activated as a student goes through the process of word learning and usage. More than rote learning is involved when vocabulary is studied in a context of meaning. Students grow in fluency and comprehension as they enlarge their vocabularies. Willis (2008) approaches vocabulary building through focus on three components, using strategies that resonate, reinforce, and provide rehearsal.

According to Willis (2008), "The brain first recognizes the sensory input from seeing, hearing, and visualizing in separate but interrelated regions" (81). When students start to manipulate the words the sensory responses start to connect to higher cortical functions. The active process of manipulating the words through activities such as graphic organizers or acting out the words brings student ownership of the new word.

When students have ownership of the word, they begin to create new links in their neuron network, which then connects the new word to similar words in a patterning and categorization process. Each of the neural networks can be constructed and activated by vocabulary building. Vocabulary building modifies brain functions in systematic, predictable ways as enriched vocabulary becomes evident in reading comprehension, verbal language, and writing. Willis (2008) posits, "Vocabulary building is a microcosm of the larger process of literacy building" (82).

COMPREHENSION

Comprehension is connected to working memory and informed by patterning. After students learn to understand the individual words they read in texts, new brain areas need stimulation and practice to recall the words long enough to understand complete sentences. The information from the beginning of a sentence or preceding sentences in a paragraph must be kept accessible while the next segment of text is read. Students also need practice storing and retrieving the content of sentences so they can comprehend pages and chapters and finally entire texts. Patterning contributes to building the memory required.

New information is gathered by the brain "through a variety of neural networks using patterns, categories, and relational connections, and builds the new data into comprehended knowledge" (Willis 2008, 127). Active working memory is needed to retain the new information. Working memory allows students to remember the beginning of a story when they are trying to read and comprehend the end. However, working memory keeps information in the conscious mind for about only ten to fifteen seconds, unless it is actively attended to or rehearsed, so Willis teaches strategies designed to build memory storage and retrieval skills.

New information or the passage of time moves information out of working memory. Information does not move from the working memory to the long-term memory unless the new information is processed by active manipulation or patterned into connection with prior knowledge. Strategies in the classroom connected to helping students remember what they read will help them connect and integrate new information into prior knowledge as they continue to read a story. Classroom strategies can build on memory storage and retrieval to increase comprehension. Children with reading difficulties, but not necessarily dyslexia, may also have poorly developed working memory.

DYSLEXIA

Dyslexia was previously understood to be a problem that caused seeing letters or words backward. Today, it is understood to be a phonological processing problem where the difficulty is with analysis and manipulation of language or phonemes so that reading becomes a matter of decoding each word. Dyslexia is a result of a functional variation in the brain. It is sometimes called a neurobiological disorder or learning disability. All brains vary, a concept captured by the word "neurodiversity." Every deviation from the norm is not a disorder. Dyslexia exists on a continuum from mild to profound, affects approximately one in five people, and runs in families. There is definitely a genetic component.

According to Klingberg (2013), "Virtually all brain imaging studies of people with dyslexia find aberrations in the same part of the brain: the posterior area of the temporal lobe" (78). This may account for evidence that brains of dyslexics rely more on the right hemisphere of their brains than the left, although typically language and reading are processed in the left hemisphere. One successful intervention is to change this brain pattern by teaching the person with dyslexia to use the left hemisphere to break down language based on syllable type and spelling rules. Dyslexia is not a reflection of intelligence. It is important for principals to know about effective intensive multisensory interventions and training programs that allow those with dyslexia to read more easily.

CONCLUSION

In a briefing paper, Johanna Goldberg and Ann Whitman (2008) state, "Reading is cognitively demanding. Reading is probably the hardest thing we teach people to do in the education system." The goal of reading instruction should be to help students achieve reading competency. Educational neuroscience studies of learning, using the technology of neuroimaging during the reading process, provide valuable insights into how the brain learns to read and how it responds to specific instructional strategies.

The more that is learned about the brain process of reading, the more successfully appropriate strategies are developed so that students' reading skills are strengthened, along with their motivation to become lifelong learners. The continued collaboration of educators, cognitive psychologists, and neuroscientists will help students develop their reading skills. All learners deserve access to the rich world of written information and imagination that is available all around us in ever diversifying formats—from books and newspapers to magazines and an ever widening array of electronic devices.

QUESTIONS FOR REFLECTION

1. How are the reading interventions in your school aligned or not aligned with what neuroscientists have learned about the brain?
2. What learning supports does your school have in place for students who struggle with a specific reading disability such as dyslexia?
3. How aware are your teachers about brain research and reading?

17

How Can Knowing about Brain Science Improve Math?

Jamie L. Hartrich

"If people do not believe that mathematics is simple, it is only because they do not realize how complicated life is."

—John Louis von Neumann

Principals hear teachers talking about how there are kids who are really good at math, some who are average at math, and some who struggle terribly in math. Math seems to be the one subject that a person either loves or hates. However, math provides students with a base of knowledge that builds a foundation for our workforce. Students who are competent in mathematics use logical–mathematical skills that develop their higher-order thinking skills that allow for transferring information from other subject areas, such as critical reasoning, pattern and relationship recognition, and conceptual thinking.

Mastering mathematics gives students the confidence needed to enter the workforce as prepared problem solvers (Willis 2010). Topics explored in this chapter are neuroplasticity, attitudes and anxiety around math, strategies for changing attitudes and reducing stress and anxiety, and effective teaching strategies.

NEUROPLASTICITY

An approach toward reducing the stress and changing attitudes around math is through equipping your teachers with knowledge about how their brains work so they can share that with students of any age. The first concept for teachers to know and be able to explain is neuroplasticity. Neuroplasticity describes the ability of the brain to organize new neural connections and even grow new neurons (neurogenesis) within the brain throughout life. Before neuroscientists were able to use imaging technologies with living brains, the belief was that persons were born with all the neurons they would ever have. This meant that intelligence was fixed, an idea that has been thoroughly discredited.

This process of neuron growth and reorganization happens continually throughout a person's life and gives a person the power to affect, change, and increase their own intelligence (Bernard 2010). It is hard for students to believe this at first, but when the realization finally dawns and students understand that they can change their brains through consistent and accurate practice and hard work, they are transformed (Pillars 2011). This type of growth mindset is based on an "I can" attitude. Teaching students about how their brains work will build their confidence and understanding of math (Doyle and Zakrajsek 2013).

OBSTACLES OF ATTITUDE AND ANXIETY

According to Judy Willis (2010), "Before children can become interested in math, they have to be comfortable with it" (9). The biggest obstacle teachers of math will face is changing a student's negative attitude toward and/or anxiety about math. A negative attitude can be the result of fear. A student's seeing numbers on a page can stimulate the same part of the brain that reacts automatically when a person becomes frightened, something that happens for example when a person sees a bear, snake, spider, or even a mouse.

Math anxiety is real and traumatic for many students. The information-processing and reasoning areas of the brain should be working hard when students are faced with solving math problems, but when math anxiety gets in the way these areas of the brain show low activity on brain scans. A student's brain can't even begin to process a math problem when it is blocked by fear or the feeling of anxiety (Anderson 2012).

This fear is being set in motion by the part of the brain called the amygdala, which is responsible for processing emotions. The amygdala becomes hyperactive and takes over the mathematical reasoning area of the brain called the posterior parietal and dorsolateral prefrontal cortex. These brain activities are connected and interfere with the brain's ability to problem solve or process mathematical problems (Willis 2010). The brain can reverse this interference if teachers help by doing the following:

- Change a student's attitude from negative to positive
- Teach students about how their brain works
- Teach students about neuroplasticity
- Develop lessons that utilize the brain more effectively
- Monitor anxiety and take short- and long-term action to diminish it

Consider whether teachers understand the role of the amygdala as the brain's stress filter. Understanding will emphasize the importance of working to change students' attitudes toward math. When a student is stressed for whatever reason, the effect of that emotion on the amygdala (a part of the limbic system in the brain's temporal lobe) is to keep information from entering even short-term memory, the first step toward reaching the prefrontal cortex and the possibility of long-term memory.

Instead the sensory input and information are diverted to the reflexive lower parts of the brain. There unconscious automatic responses of fight, flight, or freeze effectively block cognitive learning and affect student behavior. This process also happens because of other emotions, such as boredom, frustration, and helplessness.

STRATEGIES FOR CHANGING NEGATIVE ATTITUDES AND REDUCING STRESS AND ANXIETY

Teachers can use strategies to help students change their negative attitudes. Students may have a hard time changing their negative attitudes into positive ones, but it can be done with teachers' persistence. The reality is that "when students are stressed, they can't use their thinking brains. Therefore, a reduction in math-related stress is key to success" (Willis 2010, 10). The principal needs to help teachers develop and use strategies such as the following in their classrooms to reverse math negativity:

- Hold conferences with families to teach them how to reduce stress
- Establish safe classroom learning environments—free from fear and embarrassment
- Increase participation by taking the pressure off of individual students through use of individual whiteboards for responses
- Normalize mistakes as a part of learning to reduce anxiety
- Build in de-stress breaks when students are struggling
- Build positive teacher–student relationships
- Ensure success with errorless math, a foundation-building memory tool
- Enjoy teaching
- Add humor to relax and lighten tough topics
- Encourage and accept redo assignments
- Allow time for students to retake a test (Willis 2010)

Students who are making connections in mathematics to previously established neural patterns are known to struggle less with the mathematical concepts. Students who can rely more on their memory or recall of information become fast and very accurate. The hippocampus is the part of the brain that integrates sensory inputs and relational or associational patterns for memory storage and retrieval (Witt 2011). The stronger a student's neural connections are to the mathematical information, the easier it will be to retrieve the information from memory.

The difficulties of this process are compounded when students are expected to build on these basic skills as they are introduced to increasingly difficult mathematical concepts. Students have to gain adequate working memory first to be able to retain information and retrieve it for lessons in math. Mathematics is a subject where skills and concepts are related and often build on one another. It is possible that students can master some skills and still struggle with others.

Teachers who know that a number of brain functions need to work together have the key to math success for their students. Teachers will want to have their students memorize the basic math facts and practice using memory to recall rules and formulas. Additional practice guided by the teacher with recognizing and understanding patterns and sequencing lead to the ability to use sequential ordering to solve multistep problems and procedures. In teaching any mathematical concept, successful teachers place attention on the details (Willis 2010).

Also important is for students to hear that different mathematical skills are processed in different areas of the brain. This can result in students understanding some concepts well while at the same time doing poorly on others. Often students with such differentials will be grouped according to perceived ability. A better strategy would be individual diagnosis and help to raise the student's lower understanding of concepts to the same high level of understanding demonstrated with the well-understood concepts. It would be in the best interest of all students to hold off on tracking that would narrow options and lead to "rigid career and vocational paths" (Wilson and Conyers 2013, 43).

ENCOURAGE EFFECTIVE TEACHING STRATEGIES PLUS PRACTICE

Math lessons can become complicated and full of multiple steps that students have to follow. Working memory and practice are needed in lesson plans for students to master a new math concept. It is challenging and almost impossible for students to remember every step after one lesson. Students who find it difficult to grasp mathematical concepts need explicit guidance, use of scaffolding strategies, and extensive practice to master any new mathematical concept (Pillars 2011).

It is very hard for children to make their own discoveries in mathematics, which makes a teacher's guidance important. Teachers need to be able to take a concept and break it down into smaller concepts that will help establish connections within the brain and the mathematical concept. Not only will this breaking down of a larger complex help the student learn, it will also help the teacher determine where the student does not understand something. Being able to break down a problem helps build students' ability to problem solve as well as confidence, a positive attitude, and self-esteem (Willis 2010).

Breaking down math concepts isn't any different than breaking down the letter sounds of the alphabet. Anything that will capture students' attention will add to the learning. Introducing novelty into any presentation of information increases attention. A teacher can talk with a different accent, introduce suspenseful pauses, vary word order, use different colors and fonts on handouts, or even use song to convey the ideas of a math lesson (Willis 2010).

CONCLUSION

According to Donna Wilson and Marcus Conyers (2013), "Mathematics teaching that focuses on drill and memorization creates different, less robust neural pathways than does teaching that focuses on learning by strategy, or following a sequence of mathematical operations" (42). Encourage teachers to expect that students will struggle at some point with an aspect of the process of learning a mathematical concept. Having teachers who know how to make adjustments, however, will make the difference in the students' success. Teachers who can provide expert guidance, keep a positive attitude, understand how the brain works, and stress extensive practice will create better mathematical minds in their students.

QUESTIONS FOR REFLECTION

1. Are teachers breaking the math problems into small, manageable tasks?
2. In what ways are teachers giving attention to changing negative attitudes toward math and reducing math anxiety?
3. In what ways do teachers use novel techniques to capture and hold students' attention?

18

How Can Principals Support Teacher Success with ELLs?

Patricia M. Valente

> "Reaching language proficiency takes time and requires attention to students' linguistic, cultural and academic needs."
>
> —H. Gary Cook, Timothy Boals, and Todd Lundberg

Students need time and support to become proficient in academic areas in a second language. This usually takes from five to seven years. How long does it take for second-language learners to reach "English proficiency"? Research has shown that if a child has no prior schooling or support in native-language development, it may take seven to ten years for English language learners (ELLs) to catch up to their peers (Collier 1995). Language is neurolinguistically complex. The various language levels include:

- Phonological level, crucial for the abstract categorization of the sounds of language
- Word level, where lexical processing occurs
- Sentence level for syntactic processing
- Pragmatic level, where words or sentences are contextualized and inferences are drawn
- Text/discourse level, where those sentences that make up a written text or a spoken discourse are integrated to get its general meaning or gist

Although learning English may be filled with cognitive complexity, the brain can manage. Neuroimaging at a cognitive performance lab has revealed that bilingual speakers develop strong attention skills because juggling two languages strengthens the brain system that supports attention. Executive function skills are also developed, such as organization, focus, and memory. For the ELL, a network in the brain's frontal lobe will focus the mind on English, screening out words from the first language.

SPEECH IN THE BRAIN

When learning a second language the brain uses four major regions devoted to language comprehension and production. The brain makes sense of words instantaneously, but the process of transforming sounds into meaning and then formulating a response moves through several areas of the brain. When your ear turns sound waves into neural impulses, those impulses trigger reactions from these four major regions: the auditory cortex, Wernicke's area, Broca's area, and the motor cortex.

The sounds drawn into the ear are converted to neural impulses and make their first stop in the auditory cortex, located on both sides of the brain. This region lets your brain know where the sound came from and when. It then relays that information to the more specialized areas of the brain. After passing through the auditory cortex, neural sound information moves to the Wernicke's area, located in the left hemisphere of the brain. This area turns the impulses into recognizable words and phrases, and thus meaningful communication.

Also located in the left hemisphere, Broca's area is concerned with language production and motor planning. Once the brain has interpreted the language and its meaning, the Broca's area is where your response is formulated. The final brain location associated with language processing is the motor cortex, which helps plan, control, and execute voluntary movements. This region controls the movement of your mouth and lips as they form words. After other areas of the brain handle word conceptualization and phrase formulation, the motor cortex assists articulation as your vocal tracks produce the sounds we recognize as language.

LANGUAGE AND THE BRAIN

The moment sound waves enter the ear and become neural impulses, the brain executes this rapid-fire series of events, of which few of us are ever aware. For bilingual speakers, this process involves both languages. From the first syllable heard, bilingual speakers' brains are working to identify the word. The listener's brain begins identifying any words, in either language, that could fit the sounds as they arrive in sequence. Having to distinguish between two languages can be complex, but the brain's executive functions, especially the attention and inhibition processes, are strengthened through this process. As a result, bilingual speakers become better at handling tasks that require conflict management.

Language learners gain the benefits of speaking multiple languages because the language centers in the brain are so flexible. Learning a second language can develop new areas of your mind and strengthen your brain's natural ability to focus, entertain multiple possibilities, and process information.

HOME LANGUAGE EXPERIENCE AIDS IN CROSS-LINGUISTIC TRANSFER

Schooling should build on what students already bring from home. In some cases language and cognitive skills transfer easily across languages, but facilitating cross-linguistic transfer—or explicit connection between home language and English—will aid in English literacy acquisition. The learner's first language or home language plays a significant role in learning English in terms of cognitive, linguistic, and sociocultural influences.

Taking advantage of the home language in instruction or specific texts that are familiar from the home will enhance the learning experience for children. Teachers' awareness of the relationship between the home language and English would be beneficial. Teachers could use students' literacy experiences in their home language by having children bring in books or journals to share in class. By comparing the relationships between the two languages, the conversation promotes cultural sensitivity and creates links between languages and cultures for the children.

TEACHING VOCABULARY AND COGNATES

When students are allowed to use their native language to code switch between the two languages as part of the lesson activities, they are provided with the opportunity to improve vocabulary in the second language by making a connection to their vocabulary knowledge in their native language. A helpful vocabulary practice is to label and post words for common items in the classroom. By using labels for common words used in the classroom, students are able to associate and learn specific words within a meaningful context.

Another common strategy for teaching ELLs who speak languages related to English is to teach *cognates*. Cognates are words that are similar in both sound and meaning in both of the student's languages. For example, some cognates in Spanish and English are time/tiempo, hour/hora, minutes/minutos, and seconds/segundos. The goal is for students to become aware of the linguistic similarities that might exist between their two languages.

The use of code switching, the skill of switching between two languages in the classroom, is an important linguistic tool available to the second-language learner. As students become more competent in another language, they can switch languages at different levels and for different sociolinguistic functions. Students' code switching depends on whether the two languages are grammatically similar and the students' perception of the prestige each language has in a specific community. They also code switch at home or school as a tool to participate and become members of different speech communities (Reyes and Ervin-Tripp 2010).

Principals and teachers can use code switching by integrating it into the discourse of the school community. Staff can model using code switching as their everyday mode of communication and in announcements and labeling of common school items all around the school. Code switching can help to create a linguistic environment in which children feel comfortable using their native language in the school context.

Principals and teachers can actively seek out families and parents as resources for generating knowledge throughout the school year. When the school community members are familiar with students' backgrounds they become more effective at creating a supportive learning environment that supports a range of cultural and linguistic sources for all students. The use of these practices will not only help students learn but also raise the level of prestige the students' heritage language has as part of the school community.

ACADEMIC LANGUAGE AND SOCIAL LANGUAGE

Most ELLs and bilingual learners will develop a functional level of English in the first two years of schooling, but they will need ongoing support to develop cognitive academic language proficiency necessary for academic success. Jim Cummins (1999) differentiates between social and academic language acquisition. Social academic acquisition is known as basic interpersonal communication skills (BICS). BICS are language skills needed in social situations. They are the day-to-day language skills needed to interact socially with other people.

ELLs use BICS when they are on the playground, in the lunch room, on the school bus, at parties, playing sports, and talking to friends. BICS are not very cognitively demanding. The language required is not academically specialized. These language skills usually develop within six months to two years after arrival in the United States. Confusion arises when teachers and administrators think children are proficient in a language when they demonstrate favorable social English.

Often, teachers assume that once children can communicate comfortably in English, they are in full control of the language. However, there is much more involved in learning a second language than learning how to speak it. A student who is proficient in face-to-face communication may not have achieved proficiency in the more abstract and embedded academic language needed to engage in most classroom activities, especially in the upper grades.

Academic language proficiency is very different than social language proficiency. Cummins (1999) refers to formal academic learning as cognitive academic language proficiency (CALP). This includes listening, speaking, reading, and writing about subject area content material. This level of language learning is essential for students to succeed in school. Academic language acquisition takes a longer time to develop than social language acquisition does.

Academic language acquisition isn't just the understanding of content area vocabulary. It includes skills such as comparing, classifying, synthesizing, evaluating, and inferring. Academic language tasks in the classroom do not take place in a natural context of the language community. Information is read from a textbook or presented by the teacher. As a student gets older, academic tasks become increasingly unattached to context. The language also becomes more cognitively demanding. New ideas, concepts, and language are presented to the students at the same time. Teachers must provide strategic support for ELL students as they move through the process of acquiring academic language.

Becoming proficient in a second language follows a predictable pattern for most students. Students will move through these stages as they are learning a second language. How long students stay at each stage depends on them and their exposure to and practice of the second language. The following list describes each stage:

- Preproduction: Students start speaking whatever language is spoken within their home and interact with the teacher and other children the best way they can. After a while, they become aware that their speech is different and will try to learn what they can by listening to others. During this period, they may not say or write much. This is the silent period. Learning is taking place, but not much evidence is seen.
- Early production: Students begin talking and tend to use one- or two-word utterances to convey basic needs (e.g., bathroom, book, have pencil).
- Speech emergence: Students begin to use formulaic speech or common phrases. With enough common phrases, children can appear to be quite proficient.
- Intermediate fluency: Students demonstrate intermediate fluency (BICS).
- Native fluency: At this point, students demonstrate language with proper grammatical and syntactical dimensions (CALP).

ATTITUDE AND MOTIVATION

Attitude is defined as an individual's reaction about or toward something based on his or her beliefs or opinions, whereas motivation refers to the degree an individual strives to do something because he or she desires to and because of the pleasure and fulfillment derived from the activity. According to many researchers, attitude and motivation play an important role in second-language learning. For example, Robert Gardner (1985) argues that attitude and motivation are important because second-language classes—ESL classes—are fundamentally different from other classes for a student.

Unlike other classes, students in ESL classes are faced with material outside their cultural context. They are not just asked to learn about the language; they are required to learn the language and make it part of their behavior. Gardner (1985) expresses it this way:

> There is both an educational and a social psychological perspective in second language learning. Like any school subject, a second language represents material that must be learned and, as such, ability and motivational factors will play a role in the extent to which individuals learn the material. Unlike other school subjects, however, the second language represents behavior patterns and characteristics of members of another ethnolinguistic community, not one's own group, and therefore the motivational component will be influenced to some extent by factors that affect how readily the individual is willing to adopt these "foreign" behavior patterns. We have referred to these factors as integrative attitudes to indicate that they reflect the extent to which the individual is willing to come close psychologically to the other language group. (13)

Motivation plays a central role in second-language development. When second-language learners find that the traditions of native-speaking mainstream Americans are similar to their own routines, they are likely to be successful. Equally however, if they find that the routines of middle-class Americans are dissimilar from their own, they usually acquire the second language slowly and may stop learning before they gain native-speaker proficiency in English (Scarcella 1990).

CONCLUSION

Why is growth for English learners important for our schools? Second-language learners are predicted to account for about 40 percent of the school-age population by the 2030s (Berliner and Biddle 1995). Principals can help teachers and students look at diversity as an opportunity to learn and not as a problem. Being bilingual actually benefits the brain in many ways. By defining the challenges of educating students from multicultural and multilingual backgrounds as an opportunity to learn rather than as a problem, principals can begin to shape thinking and collaborative efforts in positive ways.

QUESTIONS FOR REFLECTION

1. Is the school missing any of the school, program, and classroom characteristics that support the reading development of English language learners?
2. Are English language learners being marginalized in any way in the school community?
3. Do educators in your school assume shared responsibility for the achievement of English language learners?

V

AGES AND STAGES OF THE BRAIN

19

How Can Principals Help Elementary Learners?

Jamie L. Hartrich

"Children are born to learn."

—Wendy Ostroff

Learning begins even before a child is born. Brain cells (neurons) develop at a rate of 250,000 new cells per minute during the second trimester of pregnancy. At birth a typical child's brain will create over a trillion neuron connections, making the baby's brain more highly connected than an average adult brain (Ostroff 2012). Throughout childhood, the brain will continue to strengthen the neuron connections that are used frequently and weaken the ones that are infrequently used. This process is one reason scientists have declared the brain to be the most efficient organ in the human body (Wilson and Conyers 2013).

Even though learning is very complex, humans were created to learn. From the time children are born, their lives are all about learning. Children learn more quickly than at any other time in their lives. Young children learn without realizing they are learning and without even trying. The experiences that happen in children's lives are the foundation or building blocks for the development of the brain and have a dramatic influence on their learning throughout their entire lives (Willis 2010).

INFLUENCES ON THE LEARNING AND DEVELOPMENT OF THE BRAIN

According to Torkel Klingberg (2013), a child development and brain training specialist from Sweden, there are five themes in which cognitive science is influencing the view of child development and learning. He named these themes *map, prediction, intervention, sculpting,* and *plasticity*. As defined, these themes shed additional light on teaching practices and the development of learning for elementary age children. Because of imaging techniques, we now have a better *map* of the various functions of the brain and a better understanding of its development, unique in each child.

Klingberg (2013) believes the brain-function *map* (the first theme) makes *prediction* (the second theme) possible through considering which children might fall into a risk zone for particular problems with reading and writing. We have many *interventions* (the third theme) available to help children with cognitive problems. He wrote, for example, that we have "knowledge of how the brain encodes numbers in a spatial dimension in the parietal lobe" (143) but need to build bridges to educators who will know how to incorporate that into teaching.

Klingberg (2013) writes that the fourth theme, *sculpting*, reminds us that "the brains of children and adolescents are not mini versions of the adult brain any more than sperm contain microscopic fetuses. The brain is shaped through decades of growing and pruning" (143). Each brain matures part by part on its own timetable, sometimes with the normal developmental trajectory interrupted. The fifth theme, *plasticity*, refers to how the brain creates function but also how everything is subject to influence from environment and experiences. According to Klingberg, "The hippocampus determines how the long-term memory develops, but a stimulating environment and opportunities for exploration and learning also affect the hippocampus" (144).

COMPONENTS OF CLASSROOM LEARNING FROM A BRAIN SCIENCE PERSPECTIVE

According to Wendy Ostroff (2012), author of *Born to Learn: Motivating and Engaging Learners from a Developmental Science Perspective*, basic components that encourage and maintain learning for young children as their brains continue to develop are motivation, attention, memory, and cognition and action. A principal needs faculty members that understand the components of children's learning and are capable of supporting them in the classroom. Young children learn from everything they do because they are naturally curious. When children receive the proper support and encouragement at school, their lives will be forever changed as they become adventurous lifelong learners. Ostroff's four basic components of classroom learning will be explored in the rest of the paper.

MOTIVATION

Curiosity is associated with a preference for novelty. Children who are motivated to learn feel curious and experience pleasure in their actions. Because they are curious, they ask questions and try to figure things out. The driving force for learning in the classroom is maintaining this motivation to learn that stems from curiosity. Children who enjoy what they are doing will simply continue doing it because enjoyment is motivation enough. Children learn through exploring their world by manipulation, locomotion, language, and social interaction (Wilson and Conyers 2013). Good teachers know how to infuse motivation in learning experiences in the classroom.

Ostroff (2012) offers comments on motivation and classroom practices that particularly reflect brain science. The brain is highly responsive to novelty, so surprising students with what she calls "outrageous lessons" hooks attention and builds motivation. Because brains develop in social relationships, it is also important for a teacher to create a learning community in the classroom, use dialogue as much as possible, develop real-world learning opportunities, and create learning situations that challenge the students.

According to Ostroff (2012), other components that stimulate motivation are activities that build confidence and involve play. Play promotes brain development and is more effective than formal teaching. She advises being creative and using play to develop lessons. Avoiding high-stakes academic approaches with young children is recommended. Giving them choices in both the process and content of learning is also strongly recommended.

ATTENTION

Paying attention requires maturation and use of a number of widely scattered brain areas, all the way from the brainstem up to the prefrontal cortex. Many children rarely experience a quiet, self-directed mind undistracted by stimulation. This has detrimental effects on their growing brains. To learn something, a child has to pay enough attention to what teachers have to say or to read a book so that the information can be retained and mastered (Wilson and Conyers 2013).

Attention is the ability to filter and focus on a certain task with our mind by listening and seeing. Paying attention is one of the hardest tasks for students, especially when the world around them is filled with numerous sights and sounds. With all the stimulation around them, students have a hard time bringing certain items into their conscious awareness and ignoring the others.

Ostroff (2012) offers comments on attention and classroom practices that are tied to brain science findings. In particular she elaborates on self-regulation, movement, and executive control as they are supported by classroom practices. Self-regulation is related to the ability of maintaining a state of calmness, a capacity that develops slowly through childhood. Meditation practices can help with developing the ability to pay attention, as can being emotionally supportive of the students, teaching them to use "I" statements, and providing opportunities to raise emotional awareness.

Movement is particularly important for elementary students. The more movement that is created during a particular learning experience, the more focused and attentive the students will be. Breaks are also important to being able to concentrate and pay attention. Aerobic activity increases brain functions. Finally, executive control is the ultimate contributor to paying attention. When a student is able to display executive control even for a short time, the frontal cortex, the last region of the brain to develop, is making progress. Executive control is manifested in planning, decision making, inhibition, and flexibility.

MEMORY

Learning and memory go hand in hand. Memory, the ability of the brain to store and retrieve information, plays an important role in cognitive development. We can also describe memory as the process of organizing and placing information in various networks in real time. Our brains processes determine what is remembered and stored or what will be lost or forgotten. When something reaches long-term memory, the brain will have triggered a slightly different neural or biochemical pathway.

According to Ostroff (2012), there are four memory components supported by classroom practices: (1) working memory; (2) scripts, schemas, and stories; (3) mnemonic strategies; and (4) knowledge and expertise. Reducing the amount of content to be remembered at any one time goes with the process of breaking content into smaller steps for learning, something the students can help with doing. Working memory does not function well with information overload, so strategies such as scripts and schemas that involve talking about the content will help the students remember better. Memories are also built in social interactions. Storytelling and role-playing stimulate processing of information, as does responding to questions.

Mnemonic strategies also greatly improve memory performance and help with the repeated retrieval practice that builds memory. Teach mnemonic devices or have children come up with their own. Provide opportunities to collaborate. Assessing children's learning often and providing feedback are strategies that support memory. Knowledge and expertise are built through activities and using knowledge. Work with games and songs and hands-on learning activities that stimulate involvement. Children's brains rely on already formed neural pathways to understand new information. Hooking the classroom activities with prior knowledge or experiences is an important strategy for supporting the move of information from working to long-term memory.

COGNITION AND ACTION

Learning and cognition can be thought of as synonyms for each other, and many people do think of them as the same. Cognition is the mental action or process of acquiring knowledge and understanding through thought, experience, and the senses. The ability to learn is complex, and it involves having motivation, paying attention, taking in new information, and remembering and making the connections. Human cognition is unique because we learn from direct and indirect experiences.

The final stage of all learning is thinking about it and applying it to new situations or actions. When teachers put emphasis on cognition and action in their classrooms, the students are able to make connections to real-life situations and build their knowledge base for the future. Ostroff (2012) listed steps or facets of cognition supported by classroom practices: implicit learning, imitation, emotion, metacognition, articulation, and collaboration. Implicit learning just happens, without awareness or conscious effort, as students branch out in new areas and are provided with new experiences.

Students seek role models to imitate and look to teachers as consistent and reliable models of learning. Ostroff (2012) suggests avoiding the use of video or television in favor of live experience. A strategy for modeling is to take the role of the student and participate in your own activities and assignments. This is a way to show students you enjoy what you are doing. To learn, emotional needs must first be met.

For any learning to become memory, first sensory nerves throughout the body send information to the brain. The brain cannot let in all the sensory information, so filters exist to protect the brain from overload. The reticular activating system (RAS) is such a filter, and controls how the brain "selects which sensory data to let in through the RAS filter" (Willis 2008, 166). From the billion bits of sensory information, only about two thousand can make it through the RAS per second. When stress levels are down and the brain is paying attention, the reflective brain processes the information. When stress levels are up the information is more likely to be sent to the reactive brain. A lower, more reactive brain has a limited set of behavior outputs, identified as fight, flight, or freeze modes.

Once the sensory information passes through the reticular activating system, it goes "through the limbic system (especially the *amygdala* and the *hippocampus*) to be acknowledged, recognized, coded into patterns, and ultimately stored in long-term memory" (Willis 2008, 167) in the prefrontal cortex (PFC). "The goal for successful learning and emotional control is to keep the RAS filter open to the flow of information that you want to enter your PFC" (Willis 2008, 168). High stress will reduce the flow and be counterproductive to learning. Willis recommends using humor to create a relaxing environment in the classroom. Lasting learning comes from lasting experiences that have emotional significance to the learner. Affective experience creates meaning.

The next classroom practice that can be cultivated is to teach students about metacognition, or thinking about thinking. Keep students on track during a lesson by letting them know where they are headed, and model awareness of your own thinking. Keep expectations clear and visible, and learning will be enhanced. Related to metacognition is the skill of articulation. Work with questioning and explaining and writing to enhance thinking and reasoning. Help children form and communicate their own knowledge. Have them explain how they solved a problem, and don't put the emphasis on getting it right. Consider having the students keep a journal. Have them collaborate to develop knowledge or mind maps. Any practice that provides the students with opportunities to articulate their thoughts will develop their cognitive ability.

Finally, it is important to understand that "collaboration catapults learning" (Ostroff 2015). Collaboration enhances the odds of future solo performances being better. Convert lessons into collaborative activities, and pair children within different proximal development zones. Collaboration leads to transformation of shared learning into individual learning (Ostroff 2012).

CONCLUSION

The development of a child's brain holds the key to the child's future. Children learn through social interactions and the experiences they are encountering (Willis 2010). For children, learning is about being playful, physically active, experimental, able to take risks and try something new, and most importantly, enjoying what they are doing. Creating a school where teachers understand how a young child learns implies an engaged principal. The goal is an engaged staff who build learning environments where everyone explores, discovers, experiments, take risks, and creates effortless learning together. Collaboration is the key. The goal is to create lifelong learners who will be motivated and curious to continue learning no matter how old they are (Pillars 2011).

QUESTIONS FOR REFLECTION

1. How can a classroom be built on the premise of curiosity?
2. In what ways is the school a place that promotes collaboration?
3. How can a principal create a school culture that keeps learning lively?

20

How Can Principals Help Middle Schoolers Learn?

Stacie M. France

"Nothing can be as hard as middle school."

—Zooey Deschanel

There are so many different names for middle school–aged students such as tweens, adolescents, preadolescents, preteens, and so on. It is no wonder that sources vary in the precise grade levels and age range of these wonderful young people. Judy Willis (2012b) described middle school well: "Middle school is one of the most physiologically, emotionally, and socially stressful times of one's life. The hormonal assaults, the increasing importance of peers over family in one's sense of identity and self worth, and the brain's second biggest burst of neural development all occur in the middle grades."

WHO IS A MIDDLE SCHOOLER?

Middle school students are typically defined as "sixth, seventh, and eighth graders, roughly spanning ages eleven to thirteen" (Know Your Students). Most educational practitioners and researchers agree that there are many unique challenges related to growth, maturation, and social–emotional development that teachers, parents, and the middle school students themselves experience during this transition between childhood and the teenage years. Therefore, students in this phase of development must be treated differently than elementary students and high school students (Wolpert-Gawron 2013). With all these easily visible changes, it is not surprising to discover that middle schoolers' brains are changing greatly too.

WHAT IS UNIQUE ABOUT THE MIDDLE SCHOOL MIND?

According to Laura Varlas (2014), "Adolescent brains go through a surprising growth spurt around ages 10–13" (3). The amygdala, which functions like a gatekeeper for emotional response, especially fear, is well developed in middle school–aged people. Yet the prefrontal cortex is just beginning to mature during the adolescent years. The prefrontal cortex is the part of the brain that is considered the "cognitive control center[;] it's responsible for functions like mediating conflicting emotions, making ethical decisions, inhibiting emotional and sexual urges, general intelligence and predicting future events" (Pellissier n.d.).

In other words, "adolescents have a brain that is wired with an enhanced capacity for fear and anxiety, but is relatively underdeveloped when it comes to calm reasoning" (Friedman, 2014). With the prefrontal cortex being under construction but the amygdala fully developed, it should not be surprising that middle school students often act on exaggerated emotions with little thought to the outcomes of their actions. Given this mismatch in development of the brain, early adolescents are more susceptible to pessimism and stress (Varlas 2014). Therefore, it is worth considering common stressors for middle school–aged students. Torkel Klingberg (2013) indicated that adolescent stress typically falls into one of three categories: "(1) school performance, (2) friends and family, and (3) social circumstances" (108).

Think about a typical school day from a middle school–aged student's perspective. Don't most of the encounters in school relate to all three of these stress-producing areas? For example, a student walks through the hallway with a friend talking about an attractive classmate. There is potential here for stress related to friends and social circumstances. Then the student walks into a classroom to take a quiz, only to encounter "school performance" stress. The middle school brains are not adept at learning when stress is high, so educators must consider what can be done to help middle school students relax so that learning is increased.

TEACH STUDENTS ABOUT NEUROPLASTICITY AND METACOGNITION

Educating students about neuroplasticity is an effective way to ease students' stress and increase learning performance. Neuroplasticity is the brain's ability to grow new connections between neurons (nerve cells) as we learn or have new experiences. Neuroplasticity promotes a growth mindset instead of a fixed mindset with regard to intelligence. Because the brain is always growing, changing, and creating new neural networks, intelligence is not fixed.

Because adolescents are "changing so rapidly, they seek some sense of control" (Varlas 2014, 4). Teaching teens that their choices affect their brain development provides a sense of personal control and an avenue for belief in their potential. In fact, one study showed that teaching teens about neuroplasticity early in their middle school years produced an increase in academic performance over the next two years when the study concluded tracking the progress of participants.

Could increasing performance be as easy as teaching students about the workings of their brain? Quoted in the opening paragraph, Judy Willis, a neurologist turned middle school teacher, advocates for teaching neuroplasticity to students to show them that their brains and intelligence can change. Even more important is that they have control over how their brains change if they practice and study. Giving middle schoolers control, during a time in life when they have limited control over so many things in their lives, empowers them to choose learning and focus on academic success.

Students are never too young to be educated about metacognition, the practice of reflecting on one's thinking. After a lesson or assessment students can be prompted to reflect on the learning strategies they used to understand the content of the lesson or the questions on the assessment. Knowing about the learning brain can prompt and guide such reflection. Willis developed a Brain Owner's Manual (2010), which she shares with middle school students. One concept she includes is that their brains are RAD, an acronym for reticular activating system (RAS), amygdala, and dopamine.

The components of RAD work together. Information enters into the brain as sensory data by passing through the RAS filter, an attention-switching system in the brain stem. The RAS filter closes when stress is too high, limiting information through curtailing the ability to pay attention. The automatic brain takes over, and you are not in control of your emotions. At that point the amygdala is highly activated. Willis (2010) describes the amygdala as "where your heart meets your mind" (168). She continues, "Stress closes off the pathways through the RAS and the amygdala that direct information into reflective thinking and memory in your PFC [prefrontal cortex]" (169). For learning to take place, the new information must reach the prefrontal cortex.

Preventing this learning loss cycle includes teaching students how to focus. Calmness and alertness will allow effort and practice to make a difference in their learning and help them reach their goals. Learning practices of reflection and self-observation can break up what some call the "amygdala hijack" and result in a student's deciding to review and practice learning in a way that strengthens memory formation. At that point, the brain's release of dopamine provides the pleasure that helps cement the new nonreactive behaviors. Dopamine is a neurotransmitter that carries good feelings and is released during activities that are enjoyable. "Feel good and you will be smarter" is the message to convey.

PROMOTE INTERACTIVE GROUP WORK IN ALL CLASSES

Classes that feature well-designed collaborative group work will make learning more enjoyable for middle schoolers. Principals can contribute to learning by ensuring that faculty members realize the importance of interactive, interdependent group work for middle school students. This builds a sense of belonging to a group and being valued. Successful participation in group work builds resiliency that leads to greater success, social competence, empathy, responsiveness, and communication skills. Successfully planned group work increases choice and relevance, both of which contribute to self-esteem and academic success (Willis 2012b).

Putting students on the spot individually is not a recommended teaching strategy at the middle school age. For middle-level students, activities such as being asked to demonstrate a math problem on the board or make an oral presentation to the class can lead the amygdala into a hyperexcitable, anxious state that blocks the flow of information and reduces learning. Biologically, what happens is that a greatly heightened metabolism associated with the stress means more glucose/oxygen is being used and flooding the amygdala, blocking the transfer of information or learning.

An additional issue to consider with regard to group work is the power of cliques. Anyone who has spent time in a middle school knows about cliques. Middle school students form groups of peers with similar interests to fulfill their strong need for peer acceptance. Although students gain peer acceptance by forming cliques, they also create a social hierarchy. Ask middle school students, and they will quickly explain the cliques in their school that have power versus student cliques with little power.

HONOR DEVELOPMENTALLY APPROPRIATE PRACTICES

With thirty-five years of teaching experience, author and speaker Thomas Armstrong (2006) makes broad and general suggestions for schools and teachers that serve middle school–aged students. Implementing these strategies in our schools and classrooms could decrease stress in middle school students and aid in guiding them to academic achievement. Armstrong's (2006) developmentally appropriate practices reinforce and reflect brain science about learning. To be specific, he encourages a safe school climate and small learning communities, as well as honoring and respecting student voices. He mentions engaged learning and argues for metacognitive strategies to be integrated into all activities. He strongly supports as a basic premise that students need to know about how their brains think to be successful learners.

The other practices Armstrong (2006) suggests all reflect the importance of emotion for middle school students. The inclusion of expressive arts activities for all students acknowledges the role of art in nurturing emotions and contributing to awareness of emotions. The phrase an "emotionally meaningful curriculum" (113) articulates what will motivate students to pay attention and find the joy in learning. The last practice he lists is facilitating social and emotional growth, a goal that will serve middle schoolers well in the present and the future.

CONCLUSION

Due to hormonal changes, exposure to new experiences, and the development of coping mechanisms, the daily life of a middle school student is often filled with uncertainty and drama. In this heightened state of self-consciousness, the emotions of middle schoolers will always trump reason: the emotions of their hearts will win over the pull of their brains. By easing emotional tension through safe schools and classrooms, the emotions of middle school students will be soothed, and students will be better able to learn.

"Brain research tells us that adolescents experience more comfort and enjoyment when pleasurable social interaction is incorporated into their learning experiences" (Willis 2012 b). Therefore, group work and collaboration are instructional strategies that middle schoolers will respond well to if they judge the classroom to be free from emotional and physical danger. Building classroom learning communities that are supportive and nonthreatening will facilitate learning. When students enter the classroom, however, they are keenly aware of the social power hierarchy of cliques. When trying to create a safe learning environment, the power of cliques can prove challenging.

Information on neuroplasticity levels the learning field. Promoting a growth mindset, teaching about neuroplasticity, and dispelling the myth of intelligence being fixed contribute to understanding that all students are equally capable of making academic gains. Two primary contributions of a principal to learning are educating faculty about the learning processes in the brain, and creating a nurturing culture that supports active and collaborative learning during this developmentally stressful time.

QUESTIONS FOR REFLECTION

1. How does the uneven brain development of middle schoolers impact their choices and behaviors?
2. How is successful group work defined and how often is it happening?
3. What developmentally appropriate programs do we have in place or could we develop to support learning needs of middle school students?

21

How Can Principals Help High Schoolers Learn?

Jennifer McCoy

> "I would there were no age between ten and three-and-twenty, or that youth would sleep out the rest."
>
> —William Shakespeare, *The Winter's Tale*

Adolescents are functioning at a time in their lives of enormous physical, emotional, and mental upheaval. A person has to spend only a short amount of time with a teenager to experience the emotional roller coaster teens go through on a sometimes moment-to-moment basis. For those who teach high school students, this roller coaster becomes part of the challenge of teaching every day. Knowledge of brain research can help principals assist their teachers in engaging this enigmatic population. Focusing instruction on learning as well as social and emotional development will help them make progress toward being productive adults.

BRAIN CHANGES AND THE TEENAGER'S EMOTIONAL ROLLER COASTER

Four qualities of mind are manifested by brain changes in the early teenage years, according to Daniel Siegel (2013), author of *Brainstorm: The Power and Purpose of the Teenage Brain*. These qualities are novelty seeking, social engagement, increased emotional intensity, and creative exploration. Schools should nurture the positive aspects of each quality. Novelty seeking comes along with the reward drive, whereas social engagement results in new friendships and peer connections. The increased emotional intensity gives teens a feeling of enhanced vitality and aliveness, and creative exploration expands a teenager's sense of consciousness. All of these developments have upsides and downsides.

Additionally, according to Friedman (2014), "there is a darker side to adolescence that, until now, was poorly understood: a surge during teenage years in anxiety and fearfulness." Parts of the brain mature at different rates, some sooner and others later. Because of what Friedman calls "a quirk of brain development . . . adolescents, on average, experience more anxiety and fear and have a harder time learning how not to be afraid than either children or adults." The brain circuit for evaluating and responding to fear is located in the amygdala.

The amygdala develops in advance of the prefrontal cortex, where the executive functions reside. The role of the amygdala is to evaluate and respond to fear. This means that adolescents have a brain that is wired with an enhanced capacity for fear and anxiety but is relatively underdeveloped when it comes to executive functions such as calm reasoning, planning, problem solving, and linking information to appropriate actions. The prefrontal cortex was previously thought to mature by the early twenties, but it is now understood to mature in the late twenties for young men and even the mid-thirties for some.

Not surprising to high school teachers is the fact that the brain's reward center matures earlier than the prefrontal cortex and thus drives much of the teenagers' risky behavior. On the one hand, teenagers are susceptible to fear; on the other hand, they are drawn to thrill seeking. Enhanced dopamine release in adolescence causes teens to gravitate toward thrill seeking. When watching a horror movie, as an example, a person may feel fearful while watching the movie but euphoric once it ends. When dopamine is missing, teens may describe themselves as feeling bored, because dopamine produces such a great rush.

According to Siegel (2013), the brain's increased drive for reward is also seen in increased impulsiveness, a susceptibility to addiction, and hyperrationality. This "hyperrationality" is marked by thinking in literal terms and not seeing the big picture. It inclines teens to see benefits of an action rather than the risks. As a result, positive outcomes are weighed more heavily than negative outcomes, so the brain downplays the significance of the negative. This mindset makes the influence of peers quite powerful during adolescence. As adolescents mature, however, they become able to consider the larger context and the positive values held "rather than just focusing on the immediate dopamine-driven reward" (70).

RELATIONSHIPS MATTER

The fields of affective and social neuroscience are revealing the degree to which "learning is social, emotional, and shaped by culture" (Immordino-Yang and Fischer 2009, 312). All human beings are social creatures to some degree, but "being social" achieves critical mass when children achieve adolescence. Most people immediately—and correctly—envision teen cliques and first dates when discussing high school relationships. In reality, some of the most important social relationships teens will establish are with their teachers. Research shows that teachers' relationships with students are among the most important predictors of teen success in high school (Hattie and Yates 2014).

As a result, teachers of adolescents face the daunting tasks of establishing nurturing, appropriate environments with their students, in addition to inspiring a passion for their content *and* maintaining order in the classroom. For high-achieving students, a "safe," calm environment gives them the permission to experiment—to stretch their skills in a place where it is safe to fail. For lower-achieving students, these positive relationships are especially important and sometimes can undo damage from previous negative learning experiences. Safe, nurturing classroom environments can slow down or reduce the emotional ups and downs produced by the function of the amygdala.

The relationships adults form with teens in school settings are not only significant for creating a "safe" learning environment for students. Additionally, Hattie and Yates (2014) found that caring relationships reduced teacher stress as well as strongly indicate teacher expertise. They observe that "expert teachers, in contrast with others, were highly accurate at inferring student comprehension from non-verbal cues" (106). But these inferences were accurate only when the teacher *knew* the student. Therefore, teachers' expertise depends nearly as much on interpersonal relationships as on content knowledge.

ATTITUDE MATTERS

Eric Jensen and Carole Snider (2013) explain that "one of the primary components of school burnout among students is a cynical attitude" (5). Many students maintain negative attitudes toward school based on experiences from their earliest grades. When students struggle with learning new concepts, these past negative experiences and emotions rise up and result in additional stress that may cause the students to "shut down."

While student bravado and natural attraction to risk taking are common among teens, these attitudes do not necessarily transfer into the classroom. To the contrary, the risk of failure—in this case, demonstrating to their peers that they may be struggling with concepts—is overshadowed by social pressure or stigma. Fortunately, a positive attitude—*learned optimism*—can be taught. Just like intelligence, attitudes are not fixed. When students learn they have control over their attitudes, then they can decide to change those attitudes and associated behaviors for the better. Attitude and behavior changes will, however, take concerted effort.

NEUROPLASTICITY AND MOTIVATION

Because schools operate within a system that includes individual education plans (IEPs), 504 plans, Response to Intervention/Multi-Tiered System of Supports (RtI/MTSS)—among many other acronyms—educators sometimes run the risk of viewing students through narrow lenses of *perceived* ability or lack thereof. However, when viewing students only through their documented scores, teachers can easily overlook a major component of student ability: motivation. It is also important to remember that intelligence is not fixed. A motivated student's brain can change through effort and persistence.

Motivated students can learn and understand content at significantly higher levels than their reading scores may indicate. Furthermore, these students demonstrate more engagement and persistence when dealing with content they are motivated to learn. Facilitating motivation among adolescents can fluctuate from day to day and content area to content area. However, seeking success and celebrating small wins is a good start. These "small wins" are especially important for struggling learners and those students with previous negative school experiences. Brain research shows that success is a powerful motivator, and success breeds success.

Another motivator is finding the instructional "sweet spot." Student brains are most likely to stay engaged when instruction and activities are challenging but attainable (Hattie and Yates 2014; Jensen and Snider 2013; Medina 2008; Wilson and Conyers 2013). On the other hand, activities students consider boring or far beyond their abilities actually *demotivate* them and cause their brains to shut down. Correspondingly, struggling learners benefit especially from challenging sweet-spot engagement that takes place in a safe environment.

When struggling learners are taught watered-down curricula, the negative effect is twofold: learning does not take place and motivation wanes (Willis 2014). Part of the reason that finding this instructional sweet spot is so important is that human beings value learning for which they have invested effort. This valuing of their learning is magnified when they know others will acknowledge the effort (Hattie and Yates 2014).

COGNITIVE OVERLOAD, CONTROL, AND STRESS

Teenage brains are especially sensitive to stress. Cognitive overload is a real stress for teenagers in the process of development. "If the stress is too severe or too prolonged . . . stress begins to harm learning," Medina reported (2008, 178). Despite teachers' best efforts, severe stress, he explained, "can cause brain damage in the very tissue most likely to help your students pass their SATs" (179). Cognitive overload can result from trying to multitask but also from the pressures of high-stakes standardized tests and the bloated curriculum.

THE NEED FOR CONTROL

For adults, understanding teen motives can be a mystery at times. One moment they push adults away, and the next moment they cling to their family and friends. Independence is a risky endeavor for adolescents, often determined by their perceived chance of success or failure. However, at the core of this ambiguous attitude toward independence are the issues of control. Confident students feel in control of their learning and future goals; as a result they are motivated.

Teens lacking self-confidence do not feel in control; their motivation decreases, their stress increases, and their attention to learning can wind down. According to Medina (2008), "The more the loss of control, the more severe the stress is perceived to be. This element of control and its closely related twin, predictability, lie at the heart of learned helplessness" (174).

When students have had negative early experiences in school and lack basic skills, these circumstances compound due to the frustration of constantly accessing higher-order cognitive functions, often from the lack of automaticity. A perfect recipe for stress is created by adding to that fear of failure the desire to preserve their self-esteem in front of their peers. Then when struggling students are placed in learning environments in which they have no control, their stress continues to spiral.

THE NEED FOR QUIET TIME

Adding to teen stress is that high school students confront a flood of new materials to learn, busy extracurricular activity schedules, raging hormones, and constant inundation with electronic devices. Anyone who consistently interacts with a "connected" adolescent will probably describe the teen with a constant hold on an electronic device. These devices provide teens with steadfast sources of entertainment as well as connections with their friends—thus fulfilling their desire to be included in the latest social activities.

Technology and social media are a powerful attraction but need to be balanced with opportunities for quiet and reflection. Especially when encountering complex new material, teen brains—like adult brains—need processing time to consolidate memories and new learning. Reflection is required for new learning to move from the hippocampus through consolidation to long-term memory in the prefrontal cortex. In the absence of reflection, new knowledge is passing through only a part of their brains. Principals can encourage teachers to build reflection time into class periods whenever possible. Students' working memory needs to be protected from overload so that connections can be made with already stored memories.

CONCLUSION

Richard Friedman (2014) writes in his *New York Times* op-ed, "Because the prefrontal cortex is one of the last brain regions to mature, adolescents have far less ability to modulate any emotions." The emotion of fear generated by the responsive amygdala is associated with three protective responses—fight, flight, or freeze. Whereas this might at one time have been an evolutionary advantage, it can lead to poor decision making in the context of school in the twenty-first century. Looking deeper, it seems that "adolescents are not just carefree novelty seekers and risk takers; they are uniquely vulnerable to anxiety and have a hard time learning to be unafraid of passing dangers."

Teaching teenagers can be a wild and sometimes unpredictable roller-coaster ride. Learning about these students' brains can give teachers and administrators a better understanding of why the teens act and react the way they do. Understanding teen motivators and demotivators can contribute toward a school becoming a positive and safe learning environment that causes less stress for all involved, including the adults.

Ultimately, schools are charged with the mission of teaching students to become productive citizens. Principals and teachers can aid the most vulnerable struggling learners, who often fall through the cracks in the system. The struggling learners are not the only ones who benefit when leadership focuses on helping students replace their past negative experiences with positive and supportive high school experiences. A lower-stress, caring environment aids all learners and frees everyone to take greater academic risks and engage more deeply in learning.

QUESTIONS FOR REFLECTION

1. How can a principal contribute to helping faculty accentuate the positive qualities of teenagers?
2. In what ways can a principal's leadership reduce stress and cognitive overload?
3. How can a principal help the students who are falling through the cracks?

VI
INSIDE THE BRAIN OF A PRINCIPAL

22

How Do Principals Maintain Mindfulness in Challenging Times?

Christine Paxson

> "We are great weavers of tales, listening intently around the campfire to see which stories best capture our imagination and the experience of our lives."
>
> —Margaret J. Wheatley

Mindfulness is both a word and a movement. Part of everyday life for principals is being mindful of the continued challenges schools are facing, such as state and national mandates, typically without funding. According to the 1987 *Collins Dictionary*, the word *mindful* implies "being heedful and staying aware." In that dictionary, the word *mindfulness* does not exist. The mindfulness movement, however, is both ancient and very much alive today. Across the United States and internationally, the popularity of the practice of mindfulness is one response to the complexity of the twenty-first century in education and other arenas of modern life.

Mindfulness has its roots in Buddhist meditation. It has long been thought of as an aspect of consciousness that promotes well-being. Mindfulness practices are gathering force and stature as part of a growing movement to bring neuroscientific perspectives to the practice of leadership and leadership development. The NeuroLeadership Institute and the Center for Creative Leadership are two prominent organizations supporting this cause.

THE MINDFULNESS MOVEMENT

The movement to teach mindfulness practices in schools is strong, and many leaders are using mindfulness practices to create a heightened sense of awareness of their own thoughts and behaviors relative to all kinds of situations (Marzano, Marzano, and Pickering 2003). If one defines leadership as a way of being, then mindfulness cultivates awareness that includes "paying attention to habits and barriers in the context of self and others" (Romano 2014, 7). Mindfulness has been popularized in the West by Jon Kabat-Zinn through a secular Mindfulness-Based Stress Reduction program he launched at the University of Massachusetts Medical School in 1979. A New York–based organization, Mindfulness in Schools Project (mindfulnessinschools.org) also offers training in mindfulness across the United States and internationally.

In 2010, educators in the San Francisco Bay Area started a program called Mindful Schools (mindfulschools.org) to offer online mindfulness training to teachers so they could equip children to concentrate in their classrooms and deal with stress. Their programs have reached more than 300,000 students. Educators in forty-three countries and forty-eight states have taken their online courses.

PRACTICING MINDFULNESS

There are many approaches to the practice of mindfulness. The practice can be formal or informal. Mindfulness practices are a way to recharge, build capacity to listen with empathy, be present, and attend to the needs of the staff. "Science indicates that spending five to fifteen minutes a day [practicing mindfulness] helps build a familiarity in your nervous system with calm or stillness" (McKibben 2014b). This self-awareness practice deactivates the nervous system and allows administrators and teachers to build capacity.

The Mindful School Leader: Practices to Transform Your Leadership and School (Brown and Olson 2015) is a resource for educational leaders struggling to respond to today's complex environment, where often they are expected to offer immediate responses. "This complexity, immediacy, overabundance of information, and potential for distraction has consequences for everyone" (3), but the pressure on school leaders is particularly great because they are expected to lead and show the way forward during a time when the education sector is undergoing groundbreaking change.

We have become accustomed to stress in the form of cognitive overload and a state of "continuous partial attention." Because of the brain's plasticity, practicing mindfulness meditations can reduce stress within eight weeks. A mindfulness practice actually sculpts the brain to be more adaptive to the leadership challenges of today. Educational leadership programs are just now beginning to offer mindfulness studies to students.

In the words of Valerie Brown and Kirsten Olson, "Mindfulness . . . is a thoroughly secular set of practices and way of being and growing ourselves as educational leaders" (30). Their book offers many helpful aids and protocols for mindfulness practices as well as word portraits of twenty educational leaders who describe how their lives and leadership practices have been transformed by the practice of mindfulness. There are directions for both informal and formal mindfulness practices and an informative Facebook page (https://www.facebook.com/TheMindfulSchoolLeader).

BENEFITS OF MINDFULNESS

One of the educators featured in the *The Mindful School Leader* commented on the gifts of mindfulness: "I am able to accept unpleasant thoughts without grasping, and I am much less reactive and more empathetic. I am more patient, and I enjoy my life more" (Brown and Olson 2015, 147). Based on their experiences in working with educational leaders, Brown and Olson describe four direct benefits of mindfulness to leaders:

- Improved ability to notice and slow down, or stop, automatic reactions
- Increased capacity to respond to complex and difficult situations

- Ability to see situations more clearly, or many dimensions of a situation
- Becoming more creative at designing solutions to complex dilemmas (10–11)

Mindfulness training changes not only thinking but also the physical structure of your brain. Two examples of benefits to the brain from mindfulness practice changes reported by Brown and Olson (2015) are:

- Mindfulness practice increases brain tissue in the insula, a part of the brain that supports self-awareness and empathy for the emotions of others, and in the PFC (prefrontal cortex), which helps regulate emotions.
- Mindfulness practice reduces activation in the amygdala in response to negative emotions. (56)

Another example of positive brain change after practicing mindfulness meditation is an increase in the density of gray matter, as reported from research at Massachusetts General Hospital: "The density of gray matter increased in regions governing such distinctly different activities as memory, self-awareness, and compassion, and decreased in the amygdala—the part of the brain associated with fear and stress" (Schatz 2011).

BEING MINDFUL

What principals think and do matters. Principals must respect the power of their thoughts and deeds, and realize how much influence they have. Administrators need to help teachers manage the current state and federal mandates to be productive in their classrooms. Being mindful can help a principal guide the implementation of mandates such as Common Core State Standards, standards-based grading, the assessment Partnership for Assessment of Readiness for College and Careers (PARCC), and Response to Intervention (RtI).

A situation where being mindful can make a difference is when a principal must ask staff members to do something new that adds to their responsibilities. In particular, adding new state or federal mandates can push staff members to a breaking point unless the principal leads with self-awareness and empathy. The key to being mindful of the needs of the staff and maintaining a positive culture is being self-aware. Teachers are sure to be overwhelmed. Having self-awareness about what is happening allows an administrator to make mindful decisions and support the staff effectively.

The practices of mindfulness can have a positive effect on the learning environments in which school leaders must operate. If the administrator approaches the implementation of the Common Core State Standards and other mandates with empathy and positivity, the staff will feel supported. At meetings where the staff is working through the unpacking and teaching of the standards, the principal can build in cognitive breaks. Taking time during meetings to move or take brain breaks activates creativity and renews energy in the brain. Scheduling well-timed cognitive breaks shows the staff members that the principal is mindful of their needs.

CONCLUSION

These are challenging times in education. Educational neuroscientific research is changing our minds and causing questioning of some long-held beliefs about how people learn. A new paradigm is emerging. Advocates for mindfulness training are putting well-being and compassion at the center of a new educational vision. Administrators need to nurture staff members so they can grow as learners and teachers. Principals are called to be mindful and adjust whatever they can when the stress of deadlines and of the moment seem overwhelming. Principals can nurture themselves by taking the time to learn about and practice mindfulness. Leadership can become "a way of being" for mindfulness practitioners.

QUESTIONS FOR REFLECTION

1. How might mindfulness practices enhance your leadership ability?
2. How would your school be different if mindfulness were part of the curriculum?
3. What benefits of mindfulness are of most interest to you?

23

How Can Principals Support Environments That Cultivate Learning?

Christine Paxson

"A great person attracts great people and knows how to hold them together."

—Johann Wolfgang Von Goethe

Of all the questions asked about being a school leader, how to support environments that cultivate learning is one to continually ask oneself. The question reminds principals to be reflective about a building's leadership and how it contributes to the environment in which the faculty and staff work. A relatively new interdisciplinary subfield called NeuroLeadership has emerged that is calling together researchers who are exploring the neural basis of leadership and management practices. This field has something to say to principals about supporting environments that cultivate learning.

NEUROSCIENCE AND LEADERSHIP

Insights from NeuroLeadership research can help principals maintain deepened engagement among individuals when focused on decision making to solve problems. Engagement in the workplace describes the positive emotion that a person attaches to the organization. Among other topics under exploration by NeuroLeadership researchers are regulation of emotions and promoting ability to collaborate with others.

The field builds on insights from emotional intelligence (Goleman 1995). Research indicates that emotion, more than intellectual ability, is the factor that drives a leader's thinking in decision making and interpersonal relationships. Al Ringleb and David Rock (2009) write, "An effective leader has the ability to perceive, identify, understand, and successfully manage their emotions and the emotions of others" (3).

In working toward self-awareness and emotional regulation, a foundational understanding for leaders is that a person's limbic system can respond to feelings of being fearful almost instantly. Such arousal of the limbic system impacts both thinking and performance and can automatically activate the fight, flight, or freeze reaction. This reality makes emotional regulation both difficult and imperative. Leadership that reduces the threats inherent in school as a workplace and incorporates social activities that allow for bonding will be supporting a positive environment.

Daniel Goleman, Richard Boyatzis, and Annie McKee (2002) specifically relate qualities of emotional intelligence to leadership in their book, *Primal Leadership*. They identify leadership competencies in four categories: self-awareness, self-management, social awareness, and relationship management. Each competency supports the ability to manage change. Ringleb and Rock (2008) state, "Leadership researchers have come to understand that managing emotions does not mean suppressing or denying them, but rather means understanding and using that understanding to deal with situations productively" (6).

These and other key attributes of NeuroLeadership can assist with facilitating change in schools. The goal of NeuroLeadership is to improve leaders' effectiveness within institutions and organizations "by developing a science for leadership and leadership development that directly takes into account the physiology of the mind and the brain" (Ringleb and Rock 2008, 1).

BALANCING WORK AND FAMILY

Helping the staff keep a balance between work and family supports an environment that cultivates learning. Naomi Eisenberger and Matthew Lieberman (2004) write, "Brain scans are clearly showing there is relatively little difference between physical pain and social pain." Social pain, if ignored, will take a serious toll on one's mind and body. This in turn can become very difficult to deal with in the workplace. Principals and administrators must ask themselves some crucial questions in regard to the staff when preparing for the daily routines at school (see figure 23.1 for examples of such crucial questions).

OPENNESS TO CHANGE

Remembering that human intelligence is malleable is important when reflecting on a staff's capacity. Everyone can change and grow throughout life, meaning that a staff's capacity for change can develop through new exposures or by looking at things in different ways. The

How can I help my staff learn?	• Am I providing a stable and predictable workplace?
	• Am I creating a workplace that is positive?
	• Am I mindful of the environment?
	• Am I creating opportunities to learn?
	• Am I inspiring others to grow?
	• Am I being reflective with my leadership?
	• Am I developing relational trust?
	• Am I structuring meaningful meetings?
	• Am I framing their opportunities for growth in a way that is manageable and not overwhelming?
	• Am I clearly communicating the expectations?

Figure 23.1. Questions We Should Ask Ourselves as Leaders

concept of brain plasticity tells us that adapting is what the brain does best. When a school commits to becoming a professional learning community, principals have the opportunity to provide meaningful and sustained professional development experiences that support the staff's capacity for change.

Principals can encourage both students and teachers to be open to new experiences and welcome their mistakes as part of a learning path. Since the brain is plastic or malleable, these new experiences lead to learning that results in physical structural changes that increase the numbers of neural networks in the brain. Brains change in this way across the entire life span. Helping staff continue to take risks, and feel safe doing it, strengthens key traits of high-quality teachers. The call for change in schools is constant, a given for principals who want to stay on the leading edge of quality.

PRACTICING SOCIAL AWARENESS

The craft of collaboration is essential in a school and depends on being socially aware. This is why during a hiring process an administrator is looking for candidates who can work well with others and are team players. Ringleb and Rock (2008) write, "Within the leadership literature, social awareness relates to one's ability to understand others—socially aware leaders practice empathy, which means being able to put oneself in other people's shoes, sense their emotions, and understand their perspective" (7).

Principals who strive to be empathetic can make sense of complex situations and do what is best for the staff, students, and school community. An administrator needs to be socially aware to react appropriately to situations, facial expressions, body language, and the sound in someone's voice. All of these social skills attributes can help a principal understand and adapt to another person's perspective and act appropriately.

LIMITING THE SCHOOL WORKDAY

Supporting an environment that cultivates learning requires that an administrator understand how the increased use of e-mail, texting, and video conferencing can impact a school (Ringleb and Rock 2008). It is easy for someone to become consumed with being available at all times due to the advances in technology (Waytz and Mason 2013). Principals and teachers are a tweet, text, or e-mail away from everyone.

It is essential for principals to support faculty and staff in balancing their personal priorities as opposed to always being "tech available" to everyone. Technology has real value, but having so much available at all times can be overwhelming. Responding to technology can slow people down if a balance is not established. A principal with self-awareness and social awareness can take the pressure off teachers by encouraging them to maintain a balance with technology. In figure 23.2 are suggestions for achieving a balance with technology that will help grow the performance of the staff by reducing stress.

FACILITATE OPEN AND TRANSPARENT COMMUNICATION

School workplaces are filled with amazing teachers who look for leaders who will help maintain the balance needed for the teachers, students, and school to be successful. One way

Fueling our Brains

Avoid Multi-tasking
• Focus on one activity for 20 minutes

Create space in your brain
• Take time to reflect – write down your thoughts

Limiting Technology

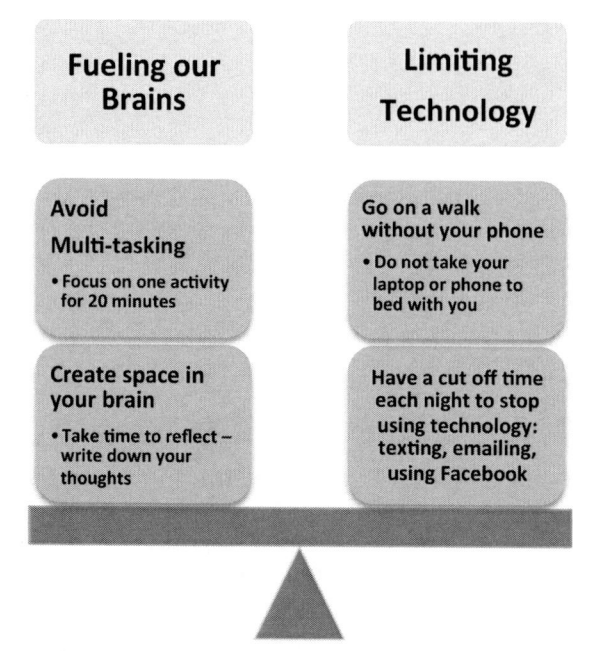

Go on a walk without your phone
• Do not take your laptop or phone to bed with you

Have a cut off time each night to stop using technology: texting, emailing, using Facebook

Figure 23.2. Keeping a Balance with Technology

principals can keep that balance and promote staff learning is by keeping the lines of communication open and providing predictability. As a principal or an administrator, it is important to be transparent in communication. An example of this would be using a Google Document as an agenda for staff meetings. This would help the principal clearly communicate expectations and procedures and facilitate collaboration.

Another option would be to use a back channel to maintain real-time online conversations during staff meetings. An example of this would be TodaysMeet. By communicating in multiple ways, principals help staff learn. Leaders may need to relay information a second or even a third time, but this repetition helps create a neural pathway in the brain (Vaughan 2014). Much like a person going on a hike, if he or she goes on the same path day after day, the path becomes one that is visible and easy to follow. Another way to help the staff members find balance in the workplace is to encourage them not to check e-mail after a certain time each evening. This allows brains time to recharge as people spend time with family and get the adequate exercise and nutrition needed to be successful. Figure 23.3 is offered as a goal.

CONCLUSION

A leader knows it is okay to plant the seed for something and step back to watch it grow into a beautiful, multiblossomed flower that is owned by the staff. Good leaders do this when they support an environment that cultivates learning. Such an environment values each person, is open to change, feels safe, and encourages and supports growth. Leaders can coach, support, celebrate, collaborate, reflect, and contribute to growth daily thanks to the neuroplasticity of

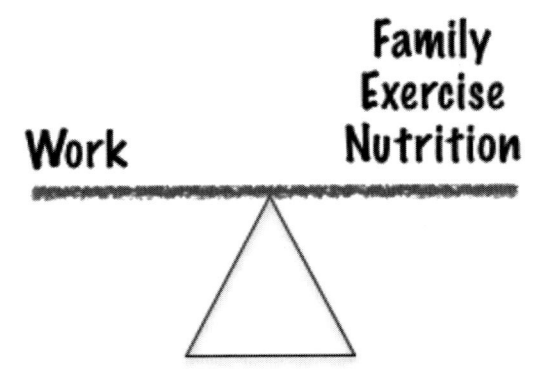

Figure 23.3. This is what work/life balance should look like.

the human brain, which continues to physically change and grow over the life span through learning.

QUESTIONS FOR REFLECTION

1. Are we creating environments that are safe for sharing, reflecting, collaborating, and offering feedback?
2. How can emotional intelligence guide a principal in daily interactions?
3. Reflect on what the work/life balance is for staff in your school. How could your leadership help the staff work together to create a better balance?

24

How Can Brain Science Inform Cultural Processes?

Christine Paxson

"A genuine leader is not a searcher for consensus but a molder of consensus."
—Martin Luther King, Jr.

High expectations to which principals are held can be fulfilled only with support from the staff. Much of the stress of being a principal relates to aligning staff and principal expectations. At any level of school, the expectations must be challenging, but within reach, for students to get the maximum benefit from their education. Getting expectations for learning on the same page also requires learning what the parents and community members want for their students.

During the school year, a principal needs to help build positive cultural processes that include and support everyone. Cultural patterns evolve over time. The leadership challenge is to keep the development moving in a positive direction. Teachers not feeling included may choose to splinter off and build negative subcultures.

Consider an analogy from brain science to illustrate the necessity for a principal to build a connected culture in a school: "To maximize potential of natural endowment of neural tissue, it is necessary to activate and exercise all parts of the brain and keep all parts connected and accessible to each other" (Sen 2010, 107–8). The wisdom about parts of the brain staying connected also applies to teachers and others on the staff being accessible and staying connected. Leaders who build connections create vital cultural patterns and processes that maximize potential.

Principals need to keep staff talking with each other so that a common sense of culture can develop. As leaders and learners, principals need to ask themselves some crucial questions that relate to their capacity to build a positive, supportive, and inclusive culture. Crucial questions for culture include:

- Am I transparent in my decision making and problem solving?
- How am I regulating my emotions?
- How am I regulating the staff's emotions?
- How do I prioritize my time at school?
- Am I allowing time to be reflective?

Paying attention to culture "can lead to better performance—not just on test scores but in the full array of social, emotional, and communal outcomes we expect schools to attain" (Deal and Peterson 2009, 4). A principal's task is to keep cultural networks positive. Culture has been called "the symbolic glue" that holds groups together and also "the web of significance." It has also been defined as something that is shaped from within, as "a pattern of basic assumptions—invented, discovered, or developed by a given group as it learns to cope with problems" (Schein 1985, 9).

A LEADER SHAPES CULTURE

A leader shapes culture through modeling approaches that reflect basic assumptions and establish positive patterns, particularly in problem solving and decision making. In the past, the emphasis has been on having a rational decision-making process. That approach toward decision making has not been altogether satisfactory. It can contribute to stressful situations when people have rational but conflicting positions on both sides of various issues. When decision-making processes are not skillfully led, people begin to argue and emotions can take over. Depending on the nature of a disagreement, conflict resolution skills are needed but may not be available. Neuroscience research has established that emotion is as important as reason for decision making. Biologically, it is impossible to leave emotion out of decision making.

When conflict arises and principals make "thinking" visible and include their feelings about alternatives, they are communicating an important cultural expectation about what and whom to include in the process of decision making. This transparent process allows the staff members and their feelings about issues to be a part of the decision making. Rather than being dismissed, they are affirmed as important and integral to the process.

In the past, principals regulated their emotions very carefully to show the control they had in the school. To show emotion was considered a weakness in a decision maker. A goal was to keep the community at the schoolhouse door, reflecting the assumption that community relations were not important and educators were the professionals in charge. Today, the emphasis is not on control but on engagement—engagement of faculty and parents and community in new decision-making patterns. Rather than retaining control, principals are concerned with how decision-making patterns invite community engagement that includes all voices, including marginalized students and their families.

To develop a more systemic professional learning community, it is essential that teachers have the opportunity to form strong collaborative and collegial learning exchanges that help strengthen their professional knowledge (Deal and Peterson 2009). Just as teachers create a positive learning environment in the classroom, so does a principal create positive culture processes within the school community. The principal who has a high level of self-awareness about emotions, and who practices inclusive problem-solving and decision-making processes, develops a more powerful learning culture that can spread to embrace students.

EMOTIONAL RESONANCE AND PRIMAL LEADERSHIP

Resonance is from the Latin word that means "to resound." In the emotional intelligence literature, resonance is used to describe when a leader and group are on the same wavelength emotionally. "When leaders drive emotions positively . . . they bring out everyone's best. We call this effect *resonance*" (Goleman, Boyatzis, and McKee 2002, 5). The ability to achieve or create resonance strengthens and enhances leadership.

The level of emotional intelligence leaders have is related to how well they are able to focus feelings to help a group meet its goals. The process begins with self-awareness. Principals who create emotional resonance even in times of stress contribute to teachers' well-being and enthusiasm for their work, both of which teachers pass down to the students. What builds resonance? In their book, *Primal Leadership*, Daniel Goleman, Richard Boyatzis, and Annie McKee (2002) write, "Resonance flows from a leader who expresses feelings with conviction because those emotions are clearly authentic, rooted in deeply held values" (48–49).

To increase morale and motivation and develop trust, a principal needs to be in touch with the emotions of the staff. From the perspective of emotional intelligence, it is also important to be able to develop a neural attunement with staff. This is also called *limbic resonance*, and is considered an attribute of a socially aware leader. Since the limbic system arousal impacts thinking and performance, administrators need to be mindful of and tuned in to their own emotions (Ringleb and Rock 2008).

According to Goleman et al. (2002), "The ability to empathize, in its most basic form, stems from neurons in extended circuitry connected to, and in, the amygdala that read another person's face and voice for emotion and continually attune us to how someone else feels as we speak with them" (48). Regulating emotions does not mean that principals are not expressing their emotions but that they can read people and situations and avoid being reactive. By keeping empathy in the forefront of their brains, principals are able to manage their emotions better and develop transformative capacity as a leader.

The brain circuitry that intertwines thought and feeling sets up the neural basis for *primal leadership*, a term meaning that the first and most important acts of leadership are always emotional and require emotional intelligence. Each of the four domains of emotional intelligence contains a skill set important for resonant leadership. They are self-awareness, self-management, social awareness, and relationship management. All four make a difference, but self-awareness and social awareness are the most critical. They are the basis for self- and relationship management. If a leader can't manage emotions, then relationships will suffer. If relationships suffer, the culture will fragment and progress will be lost.

CONCLUSION

Brain science informs cultural processes by illuminating the interconnectedness of thought and emotion in the very structure of the brain. Leaders and teachers grounded in brain fundamentals share important assumptions. Included in the shared assumptions are, for example, the following:

- Intelligence is not fixed at birth.
- Everyone can grow smarter through effort and persistence.
- The amygdala can take over parts of the brain—including rational centers in the neocortex—when a threat is sensed.
- Failure is a path to learning and growth.
- Multitasking is a myth.
- Stress is harmful to health and learning.
- Sleep is vital to learning.

- The arts nurture emotion and build emotional connections within and to school community.

As leaders reflect on their own needs, as well as the needs of the staff, clearly building emotional intelligence and fostering a growth mindset will allow the capacity of a school to grow. Teachers with a growth mindset know that their own intelligence is growing and they are adding knowledge and skills to their repertoires. By committing to building a growth-oriented, positive culture and processes in a school, the principal is affirming the intelligence and abilities of the staff. Such affirmation is a crucial motivator for the times when negative emotion and stress can impede learning. "Gifted leadership occurs where heart and head—feeling and thought—meet" (Goleman et al. 2002, 26). These are the two wings that allow a leader to soar.

QUESTIONS FOR REFLECTION

1. In what ways do you reflect on the day's events?
2. How does your leadership reflect emotional intelligence?
3. When as a leader have you been able to achieve *limbic resonance* with your staff?

Conclusion

Linda L. Lyman

"Successful educational reform and pedagogy require that teachers become culturally and neuroscientifically literate."

—Jiaxian Zhou and Kurt W. Fischer

Despite widespread interest in the applications of educational neuroscience to learning in schools, ambivalence still exists among educators about how much of what has been learned by neuroscientists can be applied in classrooms. A conversation continues to take place between the early adopters—educators who have pursued this learning and are experiencing the benefits—and those who are comfortable with the status quo.

This book was designed to be a source of introductory information for principals and school leaders about applications of educational neuroscience for leadership of learning. Neuroscientifically literate principals can use the information to bring more teachers into fuller understanding of the complexity of learning and the brain. Teachers also must become neuroscientifically literate if applications of educational neuroscience findings to learning are to occur.

NATIONAL SURVEY OF BELIEFS AND ATTITUDES

As part of my own growing interest in these issues, and part of the impetus for this book, I conducted a national survey exploring attitudes and beliefs about educational neuroscience among leaders of educational administration programs. The purpose of the survey of college and university educational leadership department chairs was to discover the prevailing attitudes and beliefs in the field about the significance of what neuroscientists can teach us about learning.

This brief preliminary inquiry into whether, how, and why principal preparation programs include and teach findings about learning and the brain revealed some of the tough issues facing the field of educational neuroscience on the level of leadership. For example, although 41.5 percent of the respondents rated the topic as "Greatly Important," this was not consistent with application. Over a third of responders indicated that educational neuroscience findings had only "Minimal Emphasis" in the curriculum for their programs, and over 50 percent characterized the knowledge of their faculty about educational neuroscience findings as merely "Fair."

Even more telling as an indicator that educational neuroscience findings are not a priority was the lack of knowledge displayed in the low composite rating of "Neuroplasticity and intelligence." This topic placed toward the bottom (eighth) of the ranking of ten topics perceived to contribute the most to a principal's effectiveness as an instructional leader. The topics and their ranking by respondents are presented in table 25.1. Respondents were asked to pick four choices from the ten topics offered in response to this question: "A principal's knowledge of which four topics related to educational neuroscience, learning, and the brain could contribute the most to a principal's effectiveness as an instructional leader?"

The three highest-rated topics (Motivation and mindset—76.49 percent; Role of emotion in learning—64.71 percent; and Effects of stress on learning—52.94 percent) are more familiar concepts than neuroplasticity and commonly discussed as factors in learning. For most people in the general population, including many educators, intelligence is something with which a person is born. However, the neuroplasticity of the brain and how it changes throughout life is a foundational neuroscience finding that means intelligence is not fixed from birth. Knowledge of the meaning and importance of neuroplasticity was clearly lacking among most who responded to the survey.

The leadership of a principal who is grounded in an understanding of neuroplasticity, the cellular foundation for all learning, makes a difference. Clearly, this is the foundation for becoming a learning leader. Findings from educational neuroscience make possible deeper levels of learning for all learners and enhance the potential of education to advance social justice. In the words of one respondent: "All learners being successful is the definition of social justice."

Table C.1. Composite Ranking in Descending Order of Importance of Neuroscience Topics to Effective Instructional Leadership

Ranking of topics	Responses as percentages	Responses as numbers*
1. Motivation and mindset	76.49	39
2. Role of emotion in learning	64.71	33
3. Effects of stress on learning	52.94	27
4. Creativity and innovation	49.02	25
5. Developing metacognition	45.10	23
6. Nature/definition of learning	35.29	18
7. Executive functioning	31.37	16
8. Neuroplasticity and intelligence	27.45	14
9. Identifying neuromyths	11.76	6
10. Enhancing short and long-term memory	5.88	3

*Fifty-one people responded.

THEMES IN SURVEY RESPONSES CAN INFORM LEADERSHIP

Six themes in respondents' answers to the open-ended survey questions suggest actions for leaders informed by educational neuroscience findings and frameworks. For each of the first two open-ended questions, three themes were identified through analysis of responses using a combination of content analysis and constant comparative methodology (Glaser and Strauss 1967; Merriam 2001). The first open-ended question was, "In what ways could a principal's knowledge of recent educational neuroscience findings about learning and the brain enhance learning and achievement in a school?" The three themes are listed:

- Theme 1—Consider implications of neuroscience findings throughout all aspects of the system when leading decision making to influence learning and achievement for all students
- Theme 2—Establish a culture of professional development focused on learning
- Theme 3—Own and model the knowledge about learning and the brain with a focus on meeting the needs of students

The second open-ended question was, "In what ways could a principal's knowledge of recent educational neuroscience findings about learning and the brain contribute to social justice in a school?" The three themes are listed:

- Theme 4—Create an optimal learning environment that allows for greater individual differentiation, reflecting a multiperspective understanding of factors that influence learning and honoring neurodiversity (every brain is different) and other student diversities
- Theme 5—Communicate that intelligence is not fixed and how neuroplasticity makes it possible for all students to learn and achieve successfully
- Theme 6—Deepen understanding of global and institutional social justice issues and remedy the misdistribution of power and influence through policy and practice

These six themes in the responses of department chairs and deans associated with educational administration programs suggest that educational neuroscience is influencing the awareness of reform possibilities. Leaders are paying attention to what some call education's newest frontier. The six themes taken together can serve as a call to action and as guidance for what leadership looks like when informed by educational neuroscience findings. The themes illustrate belief that educational neuroscience findings applied by principals could enhance learning and advance social justice.

DOES EDUCATIONAL NEUROSCIENCE NEED CONTENT STANDARDS?

The third and final open-ended question in the survey was, "Should state and national standards for Principal Preparation Programs require inclusion of recent educational neuroscience findings about learning and the brain in content knowledge standards?" The responses were mixed, with almost half of the respondents answering yes in some form, a third saying no, and the rest expressing generalized uncertainty. The diverging survey perspectives suggest that implementing new standards would be a problematic process.

Standards could help ensure, however, that educational neuroscience findings about learning and the brain anchor conversations in new places with new participants and create productive collaboration among educators and neuroscientists. The fast-paced growth in understanding of learning in the past ten years is likely to continue, fueled by curiosity, new research technologies, and the eternal quest of humans to understand who we are.

Educational neuroscience content standards would contribute to important concepts such as neuroplasticity, neurogenesis, and neurodiversity being consistently addressed in preparation programs. Principals prepared with these broadened perspectives on how learning happens will engage teachers differently in their mutual task of leading learning. Students will benefit from schools that support a growth mindset, teach students metacognitive processes, build positive caring environments, and liberate them to be learners.

The question is how to take action to ensure that recent educational neuroscience findings about learning and the brain become part of the education of every principal. Survey findings indicate that this will likely not come about through adoption or imposition of a set of standards. It takes time and colleagues to cross a frontier. Reaching the goal of neuroscientifically literate principals is most likely to come about as principals leading from this knowledge base share with others the learning successes of their students.

FINAL REFLECTIONS

Recent findings of educational neuroscience about learning and the brain suggest three imperatives for teachers, principals, administrators, and board members:

- First, to understand the brain and how it learns
- Second, to understand that the brain is an organ of emotion
- Third, to abandon the outdated belief that intelligence is fixed at birth

All three have implications for policy, principal leadership, and classroom teaching. Schools that engage students positively at the emotional and social levels can then enhance learning at the cognitive level.

Principals must understand and be able to talk knowingly about learning from a neuroscience perspective. Informed principals can remake the experience of schooling as they shape teaching practices, school leadership, and policy by this new paradigm. Too often, in the words of one survey respondent, "Foundational to effective leadership is knowing how people learn, but when asked, few educators—even doctoral candidates, especially those in administration and leadership—can answer knowingly." Each of us has a responsibility to share increasing evidence of how knowledge of educational neuroscience findings can make a world of difference for students of all ages and stages. Knowing how the brain works is the key to the future of education.

References

Anderson, Jenny. 2012, April 13. Making Education Brain Science. http://www.nytimes.com/2012/04/15/nyregion/at-the-blue-school-kindergarten-curriculum-includes-neurology.html

Armstrong, Thomas. 2006. "Middle Schools: Social, Emotional and Cognitive Growth." In *The Best Schools: How Human Development Research Should Inform Educational Practice*. Alexandria, VA: ASCD, 111–34.

Bach, Richard. 1977. *Illusions*. New York: Delacorte Press.

Barsalou, Lawrence W., W. Kyle Simmons, Aron Barbey, and Christine D. Wilson. 2003. "Grounding Conceptual Knowledge in Modality-Specific Systems." *Trends in Cognitive Sciences*, 7, 84–91.

Batema, Cara. 2014. Product of the Week: *Social Skills, Emotional Growth and Drama Therapy*. http://www.specialneeds.com/products-and-services/general-special-needs/product-week-social-skills-emotional-grow

Bates, Sarah. 2014, May 13. Dancing and the Brain. http://www.brainfacts.org/sensing-thinking-behaving/movement/articles/2009/dancing-and-the-brain/

Benson, John. 2013, October 5. Bilingual Education Holds Cognitive, Social and Health Benefits (INFOGRAPHIC). http://www.huffingtonpost.com/2013/10/05/bilingual-education_n_4049170.html

Berliner, David C., and Bruce J. Biddle. 1995. *The Manufactured Crisis: Myths, Fraud, and the Attack on America's Public Schools*. Reading, MA: Addison-Wesley.

Bernard, Sara. 2010, December 1. Neuroplasticity: Learning Physically Changes the Brain. http://www.edutopia.org/neuroscience-brain-based-learning-neuroplasticity

Bivall, Petter, Shaaron Ainsworth, and Lena A. Tibell. 2011. "Do Haptic Representations Help Complex Molecular Learning?" *Science Education*, 95, 700–19.

Blakemore, Sarah Jane, Davina Bristow, Geoffrey Bird, Chris Firth, and Jamie Ward. 2005. "Somatosensory Activations During the Observation of Touch and a Case of Vision-Touch Synaesthesia." *Brain*, 128, 1571–83. doi:10.1093/brain/awh500

Blodget, Alden S. 2013, September 10. Brains and Schools: A Mismatch. http://www.edweek.org/ew/articles/2013/09/11/03blodget.h33.html

Bowman, Rachel E., Kevin D. Beck, and Victoria N. Luine. 2003. "Chronic Stress Effects on Memory: Sex Differences in Performance and Monoaminergic Activity." *Hormones and Behavior*, 43(1), 48–59.

Brassard, Andrea. 2008, December 1. Mirror Neurons and the Art of Acting. http://spectrum.library.concordia.ca/976294/

Brown, Valerie, and Kirsten Olson. 2015. *The Mindful School Leader: Practices to Transform Your Leadership and School.* Thousand Oaks, CA: Corwin Press.

Campbell, Jodi. 2015. A Brief Look at How Trauma Can Cause Physiological Changes in Brain Structure and Chemistry. http://.www.kidspeace.org/Print.aspx?id=2014

Carey, Benedict. 2014. *How We Learn: The Surprising Truth about When, Where, and Why It Happens.* New York: Random House.

Cattell, Raymond B. 1971. *Abilities: Their Structure, Growth, and Action.* Boston: Houghton Mifflin.

Centers for Disease Control and Prevention. 2013, July. How Much Sleep Do I Need? http://www.cdc.gov/sleep/about_sleep/how_much_sleep.html

Centers for Disease Control and Prevention. 2014a, June 3. Water and Nutrition. http://www.cdc.gov/healthywater/drinking/nutrition/index.html

Centers for Disease Control and Prevention. 2014b, August 25. How Much Physical Activity Do You Need? http://www.cdc.gov/physicalactivity/everyone/guidelines/

Cervone, Barbara, and Kathleen Cushman. 2014. "Putting Heart into High School: Embracing Social-Emotional Learning." *Education Week*, May 21, 2014.

Chapin, Theodore J., and Lori A. Russell-Chapin. 2014. *Neurotherapy and Neurofeedback: Brain-Based Treatments for Psychological and Behavioral Problems.* New York: Routledge.

Chapman, Sandra B. 2013. *Make Your Brain Smarter.* New York: Simon & Schuster.

Chen, Ingfei. 2014, July. New Research: Students Benefit from Learning That Intelligence Is Not Fixed. http://ww2.kqed.org/mindshift/2014/07/16/new-research-students-benefit-from-learning-that-intelligence-is-not-fixed/

Collier, Virginia P. 1995. Acquiring a Second Language for School. http://www.usc.edu/dept/education/CMMR/CollierThomas_Acquiring_L2_for_School

Cook, Susan W., Ryan G. Duffy, and Kimberly M. Fenn. 2013. "Consolidation and Transfer of Learning after Observing Hand Gesture." *Child Development*, 84(6), 1863–71.

Cooper, Shelly. 2010. "Lighting Up the Brain with Songs and Stories." *General Music Today*, 23(2), 24–40. doi:10.1177/1048371309353289

Cozolino, Louis. 2013. *The Social Neuroscience of Education.* New York: W. W. Norton & Co.

Cummins, Jim. 1999. BICS and CALP: Empirical and Theoretical Status of the Distinction. *Encyclopedia of Language and Education*, 487–99.

Deal, Terrence E., and Kent D. Peterson. 2009. *Shaping School Culture: Pitfalls, Paradoxes, and Promises.* San Francisco: Jossey-Bass.

Decety, Jean, and Julie Grèzes. 2006. "The Power of Simulation: Imagining One's Own and Other's Behavior." *Brain Research*, 1079, 4–14.

De Koning, B. B., and Huib K. Tabbers. 2011. "Facilitating Understanding of Non-Human Movements in Dynamic Visualizations: An Embodied Perspective." *Educational Psychology Review*, 23, 501–21.

Diamond, Adele, and Kathleen Lee. 2011. "Interventions Shown to Aid Executive Function Development in Children 4-12 Years Old." *Science*, 333(6045), 959–64.

Doyle, Terry, and Todd Zakrajsek. 2013. *The New Science of Learning: How to Learn in Harmony with Your Brain.* Sterling, VA: Stylus Publishing.

Drake, Susan M., and Rebecca C. Burns. 2004. *Meeting Standards through Integrated Curriculum.* Alexandria, VA: ASCD.

Dweck, Carol S. 1999. *Self-Theories: Their Role in Motivation, Personality, and Development.* Philadelphia: Psychology Press.

Dweck, Carol S. 2006. *Mindset: The New Psychology of Success.* New York: Random House.

Dweck, Carol S. 2008. Winter. Brainology: Transforming Students' Motivation to Learn. http://www.nais.org/Magazines-Newsletters/ISMagazine/Pages/Brainology.aspx

Dweck, Carol S. 2010. "Even Geniuses Work Hard." *Educational Leadership* 68(1), 16.

Dweck, Carol S. 2015. Carol Dweck Revisits the "Growth Mindset." http://www.edweek.org/ew/articles/2015/09/23/carol-dweck-revisits-the-growth-mindset.html

Eden, Guinevere F., and Louisa Moats. 2002. "The Role of Neuroscience in the Remediation of Students with Dyslexia." *Nature Neuroscience*, *5*, 1080–84.

Eisenberger, Naomi L., and Matthew D. Lieberman. 2004. "Why Rejection Hurts: A Common Neural Alarm System for Physical and Social Pain." *Trends in Cognitive Sciences*, *8*, 294–300.

Eisner, Elliot W. 2002. "What Can Education Learn from the Arts About the Practice of Education?" Originally John Dewey Lecture at Stanford University, 2002. http://www.infed.org/biblio/eisner_arts_and_the_practice_of_education.htm

Elder, Gregory A., Rita De Gasperi, and Miguel A. Gama Sosa. 2006. "Research Update: Neurogenesis in Adult Brain and Neuropsychiatric Disorders." *Mt. Sinai Journal of Medicine*, *73*(7), 931–40.

Enz, Billie, and Jill Stamm. 2013. "Effective Strategies to Help Teachers Learn About Brain Development." In *Early Childhood and Neuroscience: Links to Development and Learning*, eds. Leslie Haley Wasserman and Debby Zambo. New York: Springer, 171–89.

Eriksson, Peter S., Ekaterina Perfilieva, Thomas Bjork-Eriksson, Ann-Marie Alborn, Claes Nordborg, Daniel A. Peterson, and Fred H. Gage. 1998. "Neurogenesis in the Adult Human Hippocampus." *Nature Medicine*, *4*, 1313–17. doi:10.1038/3305

Evans, Gary W., and Michelle A. Schamberg. 2009. "Childhood Poverty, Chronic Stress, and Adult Working Memory." *Proceedings of the National Academy of Sciences*, *106*(16), 6545–49.

Evans, Jenny C. 2014, November 10. How Stress Is Making You Lose Your Mind. http://www.huffingtonpost.com/jenny-c-evans/how-stress-is-literally-m_b_6064966.html

Ferlazzo, Larry. 2012, October 15. Response: Classroom Strategies to Foster a Growth Mindset. http://blogs.edweek.org/teachers/classroom_qa_with_larry_ferlazzo/2012/10/response_classroom_strategies_to_foster_a_growth_mindset.html?qs=larry+ferlazzo++inmeta:Pub_year=2012

Freemark, Samara, and Stephen Smith. 2014, September 29. Could Bilingual Education Mold Kids' Brains to Better Resist Distraction? http://blogs.kqed.org/mindshift/2014/09/could-bilingual-education-mold-kids-brains-to-better-resist-distraction/

Friedman, Richard. 2014, June 28. Why Teenagers Act Crazy. http://www.nytimes.com/2014/06/29/opinion/sunday/why-teenagers-act-crazy.html?_r=0

Gallese, Vittorio, and George Lakoff. 2005. "The Brain's Concepts: The Role of the Sensory-Motor System in Conceptual Knowledge." In *The Multiple Functions of Sensory-Motor Representations*, eds. R. I. Rumiati and A. Caramazza (New York: Psychological Press).

Gardner, Robert C. 1985. *Social Psychology and Second Language Learning: The Role of Attitudes and Motivation*. London: Edward Arnold.

Gazzaniga, Michael, Keith Dunbar, Mark D'Esposito, Scott Grafton, John Jonides, Helen J. Neville, and Elizabeth Spelke. 2008, March 1. Learning, Arts, and the Brain: The Dana Consortium Report on Arts and Cognition. http://www.dana.org/Publications/PublicationDetails.aspx?id=44422

Glaser, Barney G., and Anselm L. Strauss. 1967. *The Discovery of Grounded Theory*. Chicago: Aldine.

Glenberg, Arthur M. 2014. How Acting Out in School Boosts Learning. http://www.scientificamerican.com/article/how-acting-out-in-school-boosts-learning/

Glenberg, Arthur M., T. Gutierrez, Joel R. Levin, S. Japuntich, and Micheal P. Kaschak. 2004. "Activity and Imagined Activity Can Enhance Young Children's Reading Comprehension." *Journal of Educational Psychology*, *96*, 424–36.

Gogtay, Nitin, Jay N. Giedd, Leslie Lusk, Kiralee M. Hayashi, Deanna Greenstein, Catherine A. Vaituzis, Tom F. Nugent, David H. Herman, Liv S. Clasen, Arthur W. Toga, Judith L. Rapoport, and Paul M. Thompson. 2004. "Dynamic Mapping of Human Cortical Development During Childhood through Early Adulthood." *Proceedings of the National Academy of Sciences*, *101*(21), 8174–79.

Goldberg, Johanna, and Ann Whitman. 2008, August 26. Ready to Read? Neuroscience Research Sheds Light on Brain Correlates of Reading. http://www.dana.org/News/Details.aspx?id=43468

Goldin-Meadow, Susan, Howard Nusbaum, Spencer D. Kelly, and Susan Wagner. 2001. "Explaining Math: Gesturing Lightens the Load." *Psychological Science*, *12*, 516–22.

Goldman-Rakic, Patricia S. 1995. "The Cellular Basis of Working Memory." *Neuron*, *14*, 477–85.

Goleman, Daniel. 1995. *Emotional Intelligence: Why It Can Matter More than IQ.* New York: Bantam Books.

Goleman, Daniel, Richard Boyatzis, and Annie McKee. 2002. *Primal Leadership: Learning to Lead with Emotional Intelligence.* Boston: Harvard Business School Press.

Hannaford, Carla. 2005. *Smart Moves: Why Learning Is Not All in Your Head.* (second edition). Salt Lake City: Great River Books.

Harris, Allison P. 2014, May 8. Neuroscience and Feuerstein: A Principal's Eye on Critical Thinking. http://www.p21.org/news-events/p21blog/1411-neuroscience-and-feuerstein-a-principals-eye-on-critical-thinking

Hatt, Beth. 2011. Smartness as a Cultural Practice in Schools. *American Educational Research Journal.* doi:10.3102/0002831211415661

Hattie, John, and Gregory Yates. 2014. *Visible Learning and the Science of How We Learn.* New York: Routledge.

Hinton, Christina, Kurt W. Fischer, and Catherine Glennon. 2012, March. Mind, Brain and Education. http://www.studentsatthecenter.org/topics/mind-brain-and-education

Horn, John L. 1968. "Is It Reasonable for Assessments to Have Different Psychometric Properties than Predictors?" *Journal of Educational Measurement,* 5(1), 75–77.

Howie, Erin K., Roger D. Newman-Norlund, and Russell R. Pate. 2014. "Smiles Count But Minutes Matter: Responses to Classroom Exercise Breaks." *American Journal of Health Behavior,* 38(5), 681–89.

Immordino-Yang, Mary Helen. 2011. "Implications of Affective and Social Neuroscience for Educational Theory." *Educational Philosophy and Theory,* 43(1), 98–103.

Immordino-Yang, Mary Helen. 2015. Emotions, Social Relationships, and the Brain: Implications for the Classroom. http://www.ascd.org/ascd_express/vol3/320_immordino-yang.aspx

Immordino-Yang, Mary Helen, and Antonio Damasio. 2007. "We Feel, Therefore We Learn: The Relevance of Affective and Social Neuroscience to Education." *Mind, Brain, and Education,* 1(1), 3–10.

Immordino-Yang, Mary Helen, and Kurt W. Fischer. 2009. "Neuroscience Bases of Learning." In *International Encyclopedia of Education* (third edition), ed. V. G. Aukrust. Oxford, England: Elsevier, 310–16.

Jayson, Sharon. 2014, February 11. Teens Feeling Stressed, and Many Not Managing It Well. http://www.usatoday.com/story/news/nation/2014/02/11/stress-teens-psychological/5266739/

Jensen, Eric, and Carole Snider. 2013. *Turnaround Tools for the Teenage Brain: Helping Underperforming Students Become Lifelong Learners.* San Francisco: Jossey-Bass.

Jones, Brett D., Lauren H. Bryant, Jennifer D. Snyder, and David Malone. 2012. "Preservice and Inservice Teachers' Implicit Theories of Intelligence." *Teacher Education Quarterly,* 39(2), 87–101.

Kirschbaum, Clemens, Oliver T. Wolf, Mark May, Werner Weppich, and Dirk H. Hellhammer. 1996. Stress- and Treatment-Induced Elevations of Cortisol Levels Associated with Impaired Declarative Memory in Healthy Adults. *Life Sciences* 58(17), 1475–83.

Klingberg, Torkel. 2013. *The Learning Brain: Memory and Brain Development in Children.* Oxford: Oxford University Press.

Know Your Students: Nature of the Middle School Student. n.d. http://undsci.berkeley.edu/teaching/68_nature.php

Koch, Christof, and Shimon Ullman. 1985. "Shifts in Selective Visual Attention: Towards the Underlying Neural Circuitry." *Human Neurobiology,* 4(4), 219–27.

Kosslyn, Stephen M. 1995. "Mental Images and the Brain." *Cognitive Neuropsychology,* 22(3/4), 333–47.

Lakoff, George, and Raphael Nuñez. 2000. *Where Mathematics Comes From: How the Embodied Mind Brings Mathematics into Being.* New York: Basic Books.

Landau, Elizabeth. 2012, September 1. What the Brain Draws From: Art and Neuroscience. http://www.cnn.com/2012/09/15/health/art-brain-mind/index.html

Lewis, Tanya. 2013, September 16. The Roots of Creativity Found in the Brain. http://www.livescience.com/39671-roots-of-creativity-found-in-brain.html

Lipina, Sebastián J., and Martha Farah. 2011, June. Child Poverty under the Lens of Cognitive Neuroscience. *CROP Poverty Brief,* June 2011. http://www.crop.org/viewfile.aspx?id=243

Lopes, Paulo N., and Peter Salovey. 2004. "Toward a Broader Education: Social, Emotional, and Practical Skills. In *Building Academic Success on Social and Emotional Learning: What Does the Research Say?* eds. Joseph E. Zins et al. New York: Teachers College Press, 76–93.

Lyman, Linda L. 2000. *How Do They Know You Care? The Principal's Challenge.* New York: Teachers College Press.

Maas, James B., and Rebecca S. Robbins. 2011. *Sleep for Success: Everything You Must Know About Sleep But Are Too Tired to Ask.* Bloomington, IN: AuthorHouse.

Macedonia, M., and T. R. Knosche. 2011. "Body in Mind: How Gestures Empower Foreign Language Learning." *Mind, Brain, and Education,* 5(4), 196–211.

Maldonado, Marissa. 2014, February 25. How Stress Affects Mental Health. http://psychcentral.com/blog/archives/2014/02/25/how-stress-affects-mental-health/

Marian, Viorica, and Anthony Shook. 2012, October 3. Cerebrum: The Cognitive Benefits of Being Bilingual. http://dana.org/Cerebrum/Default.aspx?id=39483

Marzano, Robert J., Jana S. Marzano, and Debra Pickering. 2003. *Classroom Management That Works.* Alexandria, VA: ASCD.

McKibben, Sarah. 2014a, April. "Wake-Up Call." *Education Update,* 56(4), 1–6.

McKibben, Sarah. 2014b, November. "The Mindful Educator." *Education Update,* 56(11).

Medina, John. 2008. *Brain Rules: 12 Principles for Surviving and Thriving at Work, Home, and School.* Seattle: Pear Press.

Medina, John. 2014. *Brain Rules: 12 Principles for Surviving and Thriving at Work, Home, and School.* Seattle: Pear Press.

Merriam, Sharan B. 2001. *Qualitative Research and Case Study Applications in Education.* San Francisco: Jossey-Bass.

Mitchell, Corey. 2015. Catching Up on Statewide Efforts to Promote Bilingualism. http://blogs.edweek.org/edweek/learning-the-language/2015/04/indiana_lawmakers_latest_to_co.html

National Institutes of Health. 2012. How Much Sleep Is Enough? http://www.nhlbi.nih.gov/health/health-topics/topics/sdd/howmuch

National Sleep Foundation. 2014, March 26. Sleep in America Poll 2014: Sleep in the Modern Family. https://sleepfoundation.org/sleep-polls-data/sleep-in-america-poll/2014-sleep-in-the-modern-family/

Nies, Douglas C. 2014. "Train Your Brain to Be Its Very Best." *Vibrant Life,* 30(1), 32–35.

Olmstead, Anne J., Navin Viswanathan, Karen A. Aicher, and Carol A. Fowler. 2009. "Sentence Comprehension Affects the Dynamics of Bimanual Coordination: Implications for Embodied Cognition." *The Quarterly Journal of Experimental Psychology,* 62(12), 2409–17.

Olson, Kirsten. 2009. *Wounded by School: Recapturing the Joy in Learning and Standing Up to Old School Culture.* New York: Teachers College Press.

Ostroff, Wendy L. 2012. *Understanding How Young Children Learn: Bringing the Science of Child Development to the Classroom.* Alexandria, VA: ASCD.

Ostroff, Wendy L. 2015, February. Born to Learn: Motivating and Engaging Learners from a Developmental Science Perspective. Presentation at Learning and Brain Society Conference on Memory.

Pellissier, Hank. n.d. Inside the Tweener's Brain: What Insights Can Neuroscience Offer Parents about the Mind of a Middleschooler? http://www.greatschools.org/parenting/behavior-discipline/slideshows/4425-brain-middle-school.gs?page=2

Petitto, Laura-Ann. 2008. Arts and Cognition Monograph: Arts Education, the Brain, and Language. https://www.dana.org/Publications/ReportDetails.aspx?id=44250

Pillars, Wendi. 2011. Teachers as Brain-Changers: Neuroscience and Learning. http://www.edweek.org/tm/articles/2011/12/20/tln_pillars.html

Posner, Michael, Mary K. Rothbart, Brad E. Sheese, and Jessica Kieras. 2008. Arts and Cognition Monograph: How Arts Training Influences Cognition. http://dana.org/Publications/ReportDetails.aspx?id=44253

Raichle, Marcus E., A. M. MacLeod, Abraham Snyder, William J. Powers, D. A. Gusnard, and Gordon L. Shulman. 2001. "A Default Mode of Brain Function." *National Academy of Science,* 98(2), 672–82.

Ratey, John J. 2008. *Spark: The Revolutionary New Science of Exercise and the Brain.* New York: Little, Brown.

Rekart, Jerome L. 2013. *The Cognitive Classroom: Using Brain and Cognitive Science to Optimize Student Success.* Lanham, MD: Rowman & Littlefield Education.

Restrepo, Maria A., Ashley Adams, Arthur M. Glenberg, Erin Walker, and Andreea Danielescu. 2014. The Effectiveness of Moved by Reading Program with Bilingual Children. Twenty-First Annual Meeting of the Society for the Scientific Study of Reading.

Reyes, Iliana, and Susan Ervin-Tripp. 2010. Language Choice and Competence: Code Switching and Issues of Social Identity in Young Bilingual Children. In *The Education of English Language Learners: Research to Practice,* eds. M. Shatz and L. Wilkinson. New York: Guilford Press, 67–84.

Ringleb, Al H., and David Rock. 2008. "The Emerging Field of NeuroLeadership." *NeuroLeadership Journal, 1.*

Ringleb, Al H., and David Rock. 2009. "NeuroLeadership in 2009." *NeuroLeadership Journal, 2.*

Rizzolatti, Giacomo, and Corrado Sinigaglia. 2008. *Mirrors in the Brain.* Oxford: Oxford University Press.

Roediger, Roddy. 2015, February 22. Making It Stick: The Science of Successful Learning and Memory. Presentation at Learning and the Brain Society Conference on Memory.

Romano, Steve. 2014. *Leading at the Edge of Uncertainty: An Exploration of the Effect of Contemplative Practice on Organizational Leaders.* Dissertation: Antioch University PhD in Leadership and Change.

Rommelfanger, Karen S., and Thomas Wichmann. 2010. "Extrastriatal Dopaminergic Circuits of the Basal Ganglia." *Frontiers in Neuroanatomy, 4*(139), 1–17. doi:10.3389/fnana.2010.00139

Rosen, Christine. 2008, Spring. "The Myth of Multitasking." *The New Atlantis: A Journal of Technology and Society, 20,* 105–10. http://www.thenewatlantis.com/publications/the-myth-of-multitasking

Rueda, M. Rosario, Mary K. Rothbart, Bruce D. McCandliss, L. Saccomanno, and Michael I. Posner. 2005. "Training, Maturation, and Genetic Influences on the Development of Executive Attention." *Proceedings of the National Academy of Sciences, 102*(41), 14931–36.

Russell-Chapin, Lori A., and Laura Jones. 2014, September. "Three Truths of Neurocounseling." *Counseling Today, 57*(3), 20–21.

Salovey, Peter, and John D. Mayer. 1990. "Emotional Intelligence." *Imagination, Cognition, and Personality, 9,* 185–211.

Sameroff, Arnold. 1998. "Environmental Risk Factors in Infancy." *Pediatrics, 102*(5), 1287–92.

Scarcella, Robin. 1990. *Teaching Language Minority Students in the Multicultural Classroom.* Englewood Cliffs, NJ: Prentice Hall.

Schachter, Ron. 2012, December. Neuroscience in Schools. http://www.districtadministration.com/article/neuroscience-schools

Schatz, Carolyn. 2011, May. Mindfulness Meditation Improves Connections in the Brain. http://www.health.harvard.edu/blog/mindfulness-meditation-improves-connections-in-the-brain-201104082253

Schein, Edgar H. 1985. *Organizational Culture and Leadership* (third edition). San Francisco: Jossey-Bass.

Schultz, Wolfram. 2002. "Getting Formal with Dopamine and Reward." *Neuron, 36,* 241–63.

Schwartz, Katerina. 2013, March 15. How Emotional Connections Can Trigger Creativity and Learning. http://ww2.kqed.org/mindshift/2013/03/15/how-emotional-connections

Scott, Elizabeth. 2014, September 13. Cortisol and Stress: How to Stay Healthy. http://stress.about.com/od/stresshealth/a/cortisol.htm

Sen, Anjana. 2010. "Developing Ambidextrous, Connected and Mindful Brains for Contemporary Leadership." *International Journal of Business Insights & Transformation, 3*(2), 103–11.

Sibley, Benjamin A., and Jennifer L. Etnier. 2003. "The Relationship Between Physical Activity and Cognition in Children: A Meta-Analysis." *Pediatric Exercise Science, 15,* 243–56.

Siegel, Daniel J. 2013. *Brainstorm: The Power and Purpose of the Teenage Brain.* New York: Penguin.

Sincero, Sarah M. 2012, September 10. Three Different Kinds of Stress: Acute, Episodic, and Chronic. https://explorable.com/three-different-kinds-of-stress

Sousa, David A. 2006, December 1. How the Arts Develop the Young Brain. http://www.aasa.org/SchoolAdministratorArticle.aspx?id=7378

Sternberg, Robert. 1999. *Handbook of Creativity*. New York: Cambridge University Press.

Sternberg, Robert, Linda Jarvin, and Elena L. Grigorenko. 2009. *Teaching for Wisdom, Intelligence, Creativity, and Success*. Thousand Oaks, CA: Corwin Press.

Strauss, Valerie. 2015a, May 19. Should Schools Be Required to Address Students' Trauma? Unprecedented Lawsuit Says "Yes." https://www.washingtonpost.com/news/answer-sheet/wp/2015/05/19/should-schools-be-required-to-address-students-trauma-unprecedented-lawsuit-says-yes/

Strauss, Valerie. 2015b, May 20. Top Teachers Cite Anti-Poverty Programs as No. 1 School Reform Necessity—Survey. http://www.washingtonpost.com/blogs/answer-sheet/wp/2015/05/20/to

Stress. 2014. American Psychological Association. http://www.apa.org/topics/stress/index.aspx

Thelen, Esther. 1995. "Motor Development: A New Synthesis." *American Psychologist*, 50(2), 79–95.

Tokuhama-Espinosa, Tracey. 2010. *The New Science of Teaching and Learning*. New York: Teachers College Press.

Tokuhama-Espinosa, Tracey. 2011. *Mind, Brain, and Education Science*. New York: W.W. Norton & Company.

Trauma. 2014. American Psychological Association. http://www.apa.org/topics/trauma/index.aspx

Varlas, Laura. 2014. "Teaching to the Teenage Brain." *Education Update*, 56(9), 3–5. http://www.ascd.org/publications/newsletters/education-update/sept14/vol56/num09/Teaching-to-the-Teenage-Brain.aspx

Vaughan, Michael. 2014. "Five Ways to Use Brain Science to Become a Better Leader." *Chief Learning Officer*, 13(3), 36.

Wang, Zheng, and John M. Tchernev. 2012. "The 'Myth' of Media Multitasking: Reciprocal Dynamics of Media Multitasking, Personal Needs, and Gratifications." *Journal of Communication*. doi:10.1111/j.1460-2466.2012.01641.x

Waytz, Adam, and Malia Mason. 2013. "Your Brain at Work." *Harvard Business Review*, 91(7), 102–11.

Willis, Judy. 2008. *Teaching the Brain to Read: Strategies for Improving Fluency, Vocabulary, and Comprehension*. Alexandria, VA: ASCD.

Willis, Judy. 2010. *Learning to Love Math*. Alexandria, VA: ASCD.

Willis, Judy. 2012a, July 27. A Neurologist Makes the Case for Teaching Teachers About the Brain. http://www.edutopia.org/blog/neuroscience-higher-ed-judy-willis.

Willis, Judy. 2012b, September 14. How to Build Happy Brains. http://www.middleweb.com/2847/how-to-build-happy-brains/

Willis, Judy. 2014. "Neuroscience Reveals That Boredom Hurts." *Kappan*, 95(8), 28–32.

Wilson, Donna, and Marcus Conyers. 2013. *Five Big Ideas for Effective Teaching: Connecting Mind, Brain, and Education Research to Classroom*. New York: Teachers College Press.

Witt, M. 2011. "School Based Working Memory Training: Preliminary Finding of Improvement in Children's Mathematical Performance." *Advances in Cognitive Psychology*, 7, 7–15.

Wolfe, Patricia. 2001. *Brain Matters: Translating Research into Classroom Practice*. Alexandria, VA: ASCD.

Wolpert-Gawron, Heather. 2013, October 24. Brains, Brains, Brains! How the Mind of a Middle Schooler Works. http://www.edutopia.org/blog/how-middle-schooler-mind-works-brains-part-one-heather-wolpert-gawron

Worrell, Greg. 2015. Scholastic Inc., On Our Minds Blog. Accessed 5/20/2015 from http://www.washingtonpost.com/blogs/answer-sheet/wp/2015/05/20.

Zhou, Jiaxian, and Kurt W. Fischer. 2013. "Culturally Appropriate Education: Insights From Educational Neuroscience." *Mind, Brain, and Education*, 7, 225–31. doi:10.1111/mbe.12030

Zull, James E. 2011. *From Brain to Mind: Using Neuroscience to Guide Change in Education*. Sterling, VA: Stylus Publishing.

About the Authors

Stacie M. France has spent nineteen years teaching approximately 150 amazing students daily and is the science building chair at her school. She earned a bachelor's degree in biology-education from Bradley University, a reading master's from Illinois State University, and anticipates graduating with a master of science in P–12 educational administration from Illinois State University in May 2016. Stacie is a National Board–certified teacher and an Illinois master teacher. France has presented at conferences such as Illinois Reading Council, Illinois Standards-Aligned Curriculum Conference, and Illinois State University New Teacher Seminar. She was a member of the Illinois State Board of Education Next Generation Science Standards Adoption Committee and has participated in many district-based committees on topics such as standards-based grading, reading leadership, district improvement, and Next Generation Science Standards alignment. France is a creator and integral team member of *betabrain*, a STEAM event, hosted yearly since 2011. Because the brain is the hub of learning, studying and writing this book about how to help students' brains work most effectively was a logical step as an educator who strives to help students grow.

Jamie L. Hartrich has spent fourteen years as the technology coordinator for St. Mary's School, in Bloomington, Illinois. As well as providing technology support, she passionately spends a majority of the day teaching children from kindergarten through eighth grade in the areas of technology and also focuses on junior high math. She earned her bachelor's degree in business education from Illinois State University and anticipates graduating from Illinois State University in May 2016 with a master's in P–12 educational administration. Her accomplishments include leading school leadership teams in the area of technology and curriculum and instruction. Because of her love for teaching, she became empowered with the knowledge and research from this book. The realization that people are in control of their mind is hard to believe but builds confidence and strengthens learning.

Matthew K. Heid teaches high school physical science to sophomore-level students in classes such as chemistry and earth and space science at Tri-Valley High School in Central Illinois. He has a degree in chemistry with a specialization in education from Illinois State University.

As a science teacher, Heid has always had a fundamental curiosity about the role that creative inquiry plays in the learning process and how it relates to neuroscience. He anticipates graduating with a master of science in P–12 educational administration from Illinois State University in May 2016.

Jennifer McCoy has spent much of her teaching career working with diverse student populations—from teaching adult basic skills and GED students to high school honors and struggling learners. Her passion for helping all students succeed spurred her to pursue a master's degree in education in reading, resulting in an impetus for school-wide content area literacy at the high school in which she teaches. For her efforts, Illinois State University's School of Teaching and Learning recognized her as an honored alumnus in 2013. She has also been a speaker on the Common Core State Standards and content area literacy at the 2011 and 2012 Illinois Raising Student Achievement Conference, the 2013 Illinois Day of Reading Conference, and the 2012 No Child Left Behind Conference. Her most recent pursuits involve working toward a second master's degree in educational administration and foundations. While in this program, she was accepted into the Kappa Delta Pi International Honor Society in Education and received the 2014 Michael A. Lorber-Stella V. Henderson, Mu Chapter, Kappa Delta Pi Scholarship Award Endowment in addition to receiving the William L. and Creta D. Sabine Endowed Scholarship for 2014–2015, given by Illinois State University's Educational Administration and Foundations Department. She anticipates graduating with a master of science in P–12 educational administration from Illinois State University in May 2016.

Christine Paxson is the curriculum coordinator for Thomas Metcalf Laboratory School at Illinois State University. She received her bachelor's degree from Wayne State College, Wayne, Nebraska, and her master's degree and reading specialist endorsement from Western Illinois University, Macomb, Illinois, and will graduate with a master of science in P–12 educational administration from Illinois State University in May 2016. Paxson brings twenty years of experience in education as a classroom teacher in grades 6, 5, 3, 1, and kindergarten, and has been a Title I math teacher, Response to Intervention coordinator (PK–8) and reading specialist. Paxson has worked as a consultant for the Illinois Principals Association and a reading consultant for the Special Education Association of Peoria County, and has developed material that is used in Peoria County schools for Response to Intervention. She also works as a consultant for area schools on the Common Core State Standards, Standards-Based Grading, Partnership for Assessment of Readiness for College and Careers, and Response to Intervention. Paxson teaches a Common Core associates class at Illinois State University, which was created to work with teacher education faculty and teacher candidates simultaneously as they interact and learn about Common Core. Paxson has visited schools in Finland and presented at the University of Helsinki. She found the research for this book to be purposeful and mindful of the needs in a school: "A suitable mix of recognition, feedback, coaching, and mentoring can be integrated in a school to maintain mindfulness in times of challenging changes."

Brian M. Swanson completed his bachelor's degree in education from Illinois State University, specializing in physical/health education in 2011. Following, he completed his licensure in special education, Learning Behavior Specialist 1, at Greenville College. He is currently in the process of completing his master of science in P–12 educational administration at Illinois State University in May 2016. While attending Illinois State University, Swanson graduated with honors, was recognized by the National Society of Collegiate Scholars, and has received the William L. and Creta D. Sabine Scholarship in 2014. He has been an active member of the Illinois Principals Association and various committees at his school, focusing on student learning objectives, the Performance Evaluation Reform Act (PERA), and school and district leadership. Swanson is currently a junior high and high school special education teacher and was previously a K–8 physical education/health teacher as well as the district's athletic director. Brian has enjoyed being a part of this book along with applying this information to help all students experience success.

Patricia M. Valente completed her master's degree in reading and literacy at Benedictine University at Lisle, Illinois, in 2011. She holds a bachelor of arts degree in theater from Illinois Wesleyan University and a bachelor of science in bilingual education from Illinois State University. She anticipates graduating with a master of science in P–12 educational administration from Illinois State University in May 2016. Active in bilingual/ELL education for over ten years, Valente has taught in a variety of grade levels. While a teacher at Cedar Ridge Elementary, she served on the task forces for the design of McLean County Unit District No. 5 Standards-Based report card, alignment of the district science curriculum to Next Generation Science Standards, and the district bilingual/ELL curriculum development. Additionally, she serves on the school leadership team and PBIS (Positive Behavioral Interventions and Supports) school-wide behavior team, and is a teacher liaison for the district's Bilingual Parent Advisory Committee. She is currently working with an associate professor of elementary literacy and bilingual-bicultural education at Illinois State University researching new methods of teaching bilingual/ELL students in her classroom. She has organized and facilitated numerous staff development and conference presentations in both Spanish and English on teaching the whole child, team building, and bilingual and ELL strategies for teaching in both the United States and the Dominican Republic.

About the Editor

Linda L. Lyman is a professor in the Department of Educational Administration and Foundations at Illinois State University. She has a BA in English from Northwestern University, an MAT from Harvard University, and a PhD in administration, curriculum, and instruction from the University of Nebraska, Lincoln. She has taught future principals for twenty-five years, coming from Bradley University to Illinois State University in 1999. She teaches at both the master's and doctoral levels, and has edited the journal *Planning and Changing* since 2013. Her scholarship and teaching focus on leadership. As a researcher and writer, she is a storyteller who uses qualitative strategies and created "critical evocative portraiture" as a feminist pathway to social justice.

Brain Science for Principals: What School Leaders Need to Know involved students in the writing and continues Dr. Lyman's dedication to advancing social justice. Her four previous books have portrayed issues of caring leadership, leadership in high poverty schools, women leaders who push boundaries, and women leaders from around the world who are shaping social justice leadership through their actions. In 2005, Dr. Lyman was a Fulbright Scholar at Aristotle University in Thessaloniki, Greece, where she taught about women's leadership in American culture. Her research on Greek women principals led to her inclusion in 2007 as a founding member of the international research organization Women Leading Education Across the Continents (WLE). In 2011, Dr. Lyman was named co-honoree of a newly established endowed scholarship donated anonymously by a former doctoral student at Illinois State University.

About the Consulting Editor

Abigail Larrison is a faculty member of the Self Design Graduate Institute. She received her PhD in neuroscience from the Center for Molecular and Behavioral Neuroscience at Rutgers and her EdD in educational leadership from the University of California at San Diego (UCSD). Her focus in educational neuroscience is on developmental and systems-level neuroscience, in particular in relation to attentional, motivational, and emotional systems. Her work in the field of Mind, Brain, and Education is focused on informing teachers, administrators, and parents about the value of holistic approaches to education aligned with brain development.